TABLE OF CONTENTS

EXECUTIVE SUMMARY

A question often asked since the launch of the Arab Spring in January 2011 is what effect will these popular protests have on democracy in the rest of Africa. Frequently overlooked in this discussion is that Sub-Saharan Africa has been experiencing its own democratic surge during this time with important advances in Guinea, Côte d'Ivoire, Niger, Nigeria, and Zambia, among other countries. This progress builds on nearly two decades of democratic institution building on the continent. Even so, the legacy of "big-man" politics continues to cast a long shadow over Africa's governance norms. Regime models on the continent, moreover, remain highly varied, ranging from hard core autocrats, to semi-authoritarians, democratizers, and a select number of democracies.

Recognizing these complex and still fluid crosscurrents, this Working Group embarked on an analysis of the linkages between the Arab Spring and African democracy — with an eye on the implications for governance norms on the continent over the next several years.

A key finding of this analysis is that the effects of the Arab Spring on Africa must be understood in the much larger and longer-term context of Africa's democratic evolution. While highly varied and at different stages of progress, democracy in Sub-Saharan Africa is not starting from scratch, unlike in most of the Arab world. Considered from this broader and more heterogeneous perspective, the direct effects of the Arab Spring on Sub-Saharan Africa's democratic development are muted. There are few linear relationships linking events in North Africa to specific shifts in democratization on the continent. That said, the angst and frustration propelling the protests and unfolding transitions in the Arab world, particularly Egypt and Tunisia, resonate deeply with many Africans who are closely following events in the north.

The Arab Spring is thus serving as a trigger, rather than a driver, for further democratic reforms in the region. There have been protests in more than a dozen African capitals demanding greater political pluralism, transparency, and accountability following the launch of the Arab Spring. Some have even explicitly referenced North Africa as a model. Likewise, a number of African governments are so fearful of the Arab Spring's influence that they have banned mention of the term on the Internet or public media.

The democratic protests in North Africa, consequently, are having an impact and shaping the debate on the future of democracy in Africa. They are also teaching important lessons that democracy is not bestowed on but earned by its citizens. Once initiated, it is not a passive or self-perpetuating governance model, but one that requires the active engagement of citizens. Perhaps most meaningfully, then, the Arab Spring is instigating *changes in expectations* that African citizens have of their governments.

What makes these changed expectations especially potent is that they dovetail with more fundamental drivers of change that are likely to spur further democratic advances in Africa in the next several years.

Access to information technology has exploded in Africa, dramatically enhancing the capacity for collective action and accountability. Rapid urbanization is further facilitating this capacity for mass action. Africa's youthful and better educated population is restive for more transparency from public officials and expanded livelihood opportunities. These youth are increasingly aware of governance norms elsewhere in the world and yearn for the same basic rights in their societies. Rising governance standards in the region and internationally, in turn, are placing ever greater value on legitimacy while heightening intolerance of unconstitutional transitions of power. Civil society, typically the bottom-up vehicle for governance change, has grown in breadth, sophistication, and influence over the past several decades. And Africa's democratic institutions have begun to put down roots. Parliaments have become more capable and autonomous, independent media is more diverse and accessible than ever, and elections are becoming increasingly common, transparent, and meaningful.

Despite the noteworthy progress, significant obstacles to further democratic progress persist. Some 40 percent of Africa's states continue to be organized around authoritarian governing principles. Most of these regimes are sustained by their control over substantial hydrocarbon revenues and politicized security sectors. Norms of personalistic governance, furthermore, remain strong across the continent, including within some of Africa's heretofore leading democracies. In addition to stymieing the development of robust mechanisms of shared power, this neopatrimonial model has ingrained the belief that politics is a winner-take-all endeavor — undermining the values of inclusion and compromise central to democratic governance. Many African countries, moreover, are still building a common national identity around which cooperation toward shared objectives can be organized. This is exacerbated by still fresh civil conflicts in a number of African societies and the polarization and intercommunal differences they have reinforced.

While there are many competing forces at play, it is the consensus of this Working Group that the democratic calculus in Africa has changed. African populations now have higher expectations that government leaders act in a more democratic and accountable manner. There is a palpable sense that African citizens will no longer passively sit back and accept abuses of power. While positive outcomes are not assured, prospects for further democratic advances in Africa over the next several years are promising. These advances will almost certainly not be as sudden and dramatic as in Egypt, Tunisia, or even Libya — but are likely to be widespread, contingent on the starting point of each given society. To realize these gains, civil society and other reformers will be called upon to step up and champion change in the face of vigorous pushback from vested interests, regional and international bodies will need to reinforce democratic norms, election commissions will be required to become more capable and independent, access to independent media will need to continue to grow, and Africa's security sector will have to become more aligned with the interests of the state than with incumbent political leaders.

A Year of Change

Unprecedented popular protests in North Africa demanding greater political freedom, dignity, and economic opportunity have captivated the world's attention since they burst onto the global stage in January 2011. The subsequent resignations of long-time autocrats in Egypt and Tunisia, the toppling of the Gaddafi regime in Libya, and a shift toward constitutional monarchy in Morocco have dramatically reshaped state-citizen relations in this long static region. With tentative steps toward democracy, long-held assumptions of public passivity and the inviolability of stable, autocratic states in the Arab world have withered.

Meanwhile, Nigeria, with a population equal to and oil production roughly 60 percent of all of North Africa, held presidential elections in April 2011 that were widely regarded as free and fair. Exhibiting higher levels of transparency and oversight than any election since Nigeria broke from military rule in 1999, this achievement represented a major step forward in the country's march toward democracy.

April 2011 also saw the upholding of presidential elections in Côte d'Ivoire — undertaken in November 2010. The incumbent, Laurent Gbagbo, had refused to recognize his electoral loss, despite pronouncements from the country's electoral commission, the Economic Community of West Africa States (ECOWAS), the African Union (AU), and the United Nations. Defying calls for him to step aside, he instead attempted to use his control of the armed forces to hold on to power. However, the near unanimity of the international community, backed by sanctions, left Gbagbo increasingly isolated. After months of stalemate and escalating tensions and violence, Gbagbo was arrested by forces loyal to the electoral victor, Alassane Ouattara. An estimated 3,000 Ivoirians were killed as a result of the military confrontation. The case holds significant regional relevance as it paralleled episodes in Kenya and Zimbabwe in recent years where incumbent presidents also refused to step aside after they were widely perceived to have lost electoral bids and instead negotiated power-sharing agreements to keep their positions. In Côte d'Ivoire, this pattern was broken.

These events came on the heels of the reversal of military coups in Niger and Guinea that had threatened to take these countries and the region back down the failed road of military rule. In Niger, military officers restored authority to a popularly elected civilian leader one year after seizing power from President Mamadou Tandja, who repeatedly attempted to bypass the constitution to perpetuate his stay in power. In Guinea, democratic elections in November 2010 brought Alpha Condé to power, ending more than 40 years of near continuous military rule, including a 2008 coup by Captain Daddis Camara. The elections were further notable in that the losing candidate in the closely contested outcome, Cellou Dalein Diallo, graciously accepted defeat and facilitated Guinea's first steps toward a democratic political system.[1]

In short, 2011 has been a year of active democratic ferment in Africa.

It is within this already shifting context that the sensation of the Arab Spring captivated Africa's collective consciousness. Despite the major social, cultural, and economic differences between North Africa and the rest of the continent, the mass protests in Tunisia and Egypt have riveted the attention of millions of Africans from all walks of life. Expressions of frustration with political exclusion, corruption, yawning inequality, and impunity seen on the streets of Cairo and Tunis have resonated deeply across the continent. Indeed, protests demanding more political liberties, services, and accountability were seen in over a dozen Sub-Saharan African countries including Burkina Faso, Uganda, Senegal, Benin, Malawi, Kenya, Djibouti, Mauritania, Cameroon, Gabon, Guinea-Bissau, and Swaziland in the months following the launch of the Arab Spring.

These protests have mostly been short-lived, leading many observers to conclude that the spillover between North and Sub-Saharan Africa would be minimal. They reasoned that Africans were too passive, disorganized, and poor and faced regimes far more willing to respond with lethal force for social uprisings to gain traction and affect political change.

This notion has been augmented by a series of troubling cases in Senegal, Malawi, and Benin, where democratically elected African leaders have attempted to alter electoral rules, orchestrate familial successions, employ violence to break up peaceful protests, and restrict the media. This is coupled with the continued repressiveness of the region's most restrictive regimes — such as Equatorial Guinea, Eritrea, Ethiopia, Rwanda, Sudan, and Zimbabwe — where even watching the North African protests on television has been grounds for imprisonment.

Recognizing the still unfolding nature of these phenomena and the many complex countervailing forces at play, this *ACSS Special Report* attempts to discern the broader relevance of these events and their implications for Africa's democratic trajectory. In particular, how sustainable are these democratic advances? How serious are the prospects for further democratic transitions across the continent? And what, if anything, can regional and international actors do to support these reforms?

Africa's Checkered Democratic Progress

Despite its historic significance, the question of whether and how the Arab Spring will spark greater agitation for democracy in Africa has the sequence backwards. Much of Sub-Saharan Africa (hereafter referred to as Africa) realized a significant democratic breakthrough in the early 1990s with the end of the Cold War and the superpower rivalries that had artificially propped up numerous unpopular autocratic regimes. Between 1991 and 1994, the number of legally mandated one-party states in Africa shrank from 38 to zero[2] (see Figure 1). This was accompanied by an expansion in the number of democratic and intermediate (or hybrid) regimes. In addition to multipartyism, the past two decades have seen an expansion of independent media, blossoming civil society, a decline in military governments, increasingly regular elections, the turning out of longtime dictators, the precedent of alternations of power, and other facets of democratic politics emerge in Africa. Reflecting this dramatic shift in governance norms, the founding protocol of the AU in 2002 embraced the promotion of democratic principles and institutions, popular participation, and good governance. These values were further reinforced in the AU's adoption of its African Charter on Democracy, Elections, and Governance in 2007. Not coincidentally, the period since the mid-1990s has seen a 60 percent decline in the number and magnitude of conflicts on the continent and an unprecedented period of economic expansion, highlighting the important ripple effects likely to emanate from further democratic gains.

Africa's democratization experience, accordingly, predates the Arab Spring. The demands of protesters in North Africa — elections, a free press, freedom of assembly — are rights most Africans ostensibly already have. Indeed, one of the remarkable aspects of the prospective democratic transitions in North Africa and the Middle East is that it has taken so long. With the exception of Central Asia, the Arab world is the last major region to start down the democratic path.

Still, the dramatic struggle for freedom in North Africa reverberates deeply throughout the rest of Africa. For while there has been noteworthy progress relative to the previous autocratic decades, Africa's democratic path has been checkered and is far from complete. Despite the emergence of some 8 African democracies and with another 20 or so on a democratizing path, 40 percent of all African governments still have dominant autocratic leanings (see Table 1). These include autocracies that are explicitly intolerant of any opposition as well as semi-authoritarian regimes that have in theory adopted important features of democracy, such as multipartyism, respect for civil liberties, independent media, and periodic elections, but in fact do not allow genuine contestations of power.[5] In other words, they wish to garner the reputational benefits of democracy without commitments to shared power, representation, and equality under the law. Such quasi-authoritarians comprise a fifth of African regimes.

So, while there has been considerable progress over the past two decades, Africa's democratic experience has also been marked by great variance. Serious challenges to further democratic progress persist at each stage of this governance spectrum. Among some of Africa's vanguard democracies, there are still significant risks of backsliding. In fact, the number of African countries categorized as democracies by independent indices has dipped slightly in recent years. These cases pose illuminating tests as to whether still nascent democratic institutions can withstand the pressure of powerful individual politicians seeking to perpetuate their influence by undermining checks and balances on executive authority.

Meanwhile, Africa's democratizers, those countries that have started down the democratic path, often face sustained pushback from remnants of previous regimes that benefitted handsomely from access to public resources and patronage opportunities. Democratizers in post-conflict contexts confront a particularly steep hurdle given their deep societal divisions, political polarization, devastated infrastructure, and weak economies.

Autocratic regimes have largely foregone the pretense of democratic legitimacy and the international support this affords. They achieve a degree of domestic political equilibrium largely through a heavy reliance on repression. None of these governments can be considered stable, however. They are, therefore, a far cry from the brutal tyrants of decades past such as Siad Barre, Mobutu Sese Seko, Mengistu Halle Mariam, Idi Amin, Hissène Habré, Jean-Bedel Bokassa, or Sékou Touré. A number of these contemporary autocrats, moreover, face active, if weak, pressure to expand democratic space.

Africa's highly varied governance landscape, then, is also highly dynamic. There are crosscutting pressures on all regime types. The direction of Africa's future trajectory, therefore, is still very much in formation. Accordingly, as this *Special Report* examines prospects for democratic progress, it focuses on *relative* progress. It is not measuring whether and when all of these regimes will become stable consolidated democracies — something that is a decades-long process. Rather, it seeks to understand what changes underway may cause a state to shift forward (or backward) to the next category along the political spectrum — from autocracy to semi-authoritarian, semi-authoritarian to democratizer, or democratizer to democracy.

This assessment similarly starts from the perspective that the democratization experience across the globe over the past several decades is not typically linear. In fact, 55 percent of all countries that have started to democratize over this period have experienced at least one episode of backsliding, early indications of which may already be emerging in post-Mubarak Egypt.[6] Still, and importantly for this analysis, three quarters of those backsliders resumed their democratic direction within three years. In short, the back and forth along this spectrum is to be expected. Setbacks are not necessarily permanent. Nor are democratic gains — until these patterns become fully internalized within a society's political consciousness.

TRIGGERS AND DRIVERS: AFRICA'S CHANGING DEMOCRATIC EXPECTATIONS

Many of the challenges, frustrations, and unmet aspirations of Africa's democracies have existed for years now. In some cases longer. Why then is there such agitation for reform now? In other words, what has changed?

To address this question this review assesses various triggers and drivers spurring the latest push for democracy in Africa. This will help put the recent spate of political reform into perspective and better assess its implications for Africa's democratic trajectory. A unifying theme of these influences is that they have all raised the expectations African citizens have of their governments.

The Arab Spring

Many Africans have been absorbed by the popular protests in North Africa. The issues motivating public anger in the Arab world — restricted civil liberties, corruption, widening disparities in wealth, lack of dignity, police impunity, and sham elections — echo loudly in Africa. So, while there are major cultural, economic, and geographic differences, the experiences in North Africa are serving as models for the rest of Africa. Indeed, in the months following the launch of the Arab Spring, there have been protests in more than a dozen African capitals calling for greater political participation, transparency, and adherence to the rule of law. Many protesters drew direct parallels to Egypt and Tunisia (see side bar).

Most significantly, the Egyptian and Tunisian (and to a lesser extent, Libyan) experiences have demonstrated that organized, focused, mass action can succeed in turning out long-time autocratic leaders — something that had not been an option through the ballot box. In the process, African populations have had their consciousness raised over the efficacy of "people power." That is, protest is more than just an outlet to vent anger. It is a viable method to generate tangible political change.

The North African revolutions have demonstrated that the strength of citizen initiatives is their size. Mobilizing the citizenry across broad segments of the population starkly juxtaposes the injustice of an elite minority pursuing their self-interest at the expense of the majority. Autocracies survive on the passivity of their populations. If this passivity can be overcome, the legitimacy gap faced by autocratic leaders comes into sharp focus — and the relative vulnerability of these regimes exposed.

This recognition sparks public debate over the acceptable basis for claims on authority. Even though most African countries achieved independence more than 40 years ago, such debates have not taken place in many societies. Colonies were quickly transformed into independent states with little time to forge a common national identity, participatory political institutions, or a shared vision. Most soon became one-party states — a status they retained for the next several decades. Therefore, even if

The Arab Spring in Africa:

- **Mauritania:** Yakoub Ould Khatry sets himself on fire at the gates of the presidential palace shortly after the downfall of Tunisian President Zine El Abidine Ben Ali. Khatry's final post on Facebook demanded "legitimate rights," the release of activists from prison, and a constitutional amendment banning all current and former military figures from seeking the presidency. Street protests followed in February, March, and June, with calls for the replacement of the prime minister.

- **Burkina Faso:** A series of protests unfold from April through June with slogans such as "Tunisia is in Koudougou" and "Burkina will have its Egypt." At an October rally in the capital to launch a new strategy for municipal and legislative elections in 2012, an opposition party leader announced a "Burkina Spring."

- **Gabon:** Police break up protests in Libreville in January in which demonstrators carry signs that read "In Tunisia, Ben Ali left. In Gabon, [President] Ali Ben out."

- **Uganda:** The Ugandan Communications Commission informed mobile operators to intercept and block SMS messages containing the following words during the February 2011 national elections: "Egypt," "Tunisia," "Mubarak," "dictator," "Ben Ali," and "People Power."

- **Uganda:** A leading Ugandan columnist writes in September 2011: "It would be dangerous for Museveni to infer from [any] structural differences that the risk for a Tunisia-like civil insurrection is impossible in Uganda....Persistent protests in Tunisia and Egypt began almost five years ago — and see where they ended."

- **Nigeria:** A March 2011 editorial in The Vanguard titled "Don't Take Citizens for Granted" argued that "Minister of Information and Communication, Mr. Labaran Maku badly missed the point when he gave reasons for the absence of North Africa-type protests in Nigeria."

- **Malawi:** During a nationwide strike in September 2011 a leading civil society activist tells reporters, "The Arab spring has been a great inspiration to us."

- **Senegal:** A founder of the activist group "Y'en a marre," launched in January 2011 and meaning "We're Fed Up," explains during a radio interview in July announcing a youth voter drive: "We have witnessed the Arab Spring. Here we will have the Spring of the 'y'en a maristes' but in a more intelligent fashion. A democratic insurrection through the electoral system, in accordance with the law and other regulations."

the Arab Spring has not translated into large-scale protests in Africa, it has sparked an essential debate about governance, legitimacy, and the relationship between state and society.

The North African revolutions also demonstrated that freedoms are not given but earned. Nor can they be delivered from the outside. Citizens need to take initiative if they want change. The Arab Spring has symbolized the importance of citizens making demands on their governments (and therefore setting a baseline of governance standards). Absent these demands, leaders have few incentives to proactively support the interests of the general population.

Closely related to this is the recognition that democracy is not free. Egyptian and Tunisian protesters took risks that entailed the loss of jobs, income, and the status quo. Many were imprisoned and some injured or killed. The brutal violence Libyan citizens faced in reaction to their demands for change is a sobering reminder of this. This realization has undoubtedly had a dampening effect on activists elsewhere in Africa who calculate that their governments too will not hesitate to use violence against citizens.

Another key lesson from the North African protests still being digested by African democracy proponents is the degree of organization involved. While escalating in size once the initial protests struck a popular nerve, civil society activists in Egypt engaged in extensive planning on how to advance reforms prior to the start of the massive street protests on January 25, 2011. These organizational meetings brought together many divergent civil society groups, establishing ties to a wide range of constituencies. This was instrumental in mobilizing the broad base of support that responded to the calls for change. These meetings also had the effect of strengthening networks of civil society organizations in the country — a feature that has been vital to sustaining successful democratic transitions elsewhere in the face of the inevitable pushback from vested interests.[7] In Egypt, it is these civil society networks that continue to push for reform in the face of the ambiguous commitment on the part of the military government to real democratic change.

Perhaps most tangibly, having watched ordinary Egyptians, Tunisians, and Libyans challenge and topple some of the most powerful regimes on the continent, Africans are going to be less willing to accept stolen elections, presidential term extensions, police impunity, and high-level corruption in the future. Rather, they will be more inclined to turn out on the streets, protest, and engage in civil disobedience to fight for and protect their rights.

President Abdoulaye Wade learned this first hand when he proposed in June 2011 that the Senegalese constitution be amended to allow presidential elections to be won on a first round of balloting with as little as 25 percent of the popular vote. The suggestion resulted in thousands of youth coming out onto the streets of Senegal's major cities in a matter of hours. The protesters hurled stones at the Parliament building and clashed with riot police, who were deployed in force on roads leading up to the Parliament and inside the premises. The opposition subsequently announced a "Don't Touch My Constitution" coalition and world-renowned Senegalese singer Youssou N'Dour criticized the "abuse of authority." President Wade quickly revoked the proposal.

Expanding Information and Communications Technology

Whereas the sudden unfolding of the Arab Spring has been a trigger or catalyst to political reform efforts in Africa, other fundamental changes over the past decade have been reshaping Africa's democratic prospects. Key among these drivers is the dramatic evolution in Africa's information systems.[8] Tens of millions of Africans are today interconnected, globally networked, and informed in ways not possible just a few years ago. This dramatic and rapidly emerging phenomenon is having profound social, economic, and political impacts. Africans now have more numerous and independent sources of information, more ways to share it, greater knowledge about their leaders and governments, and more opportunities to express opinions and extend support to reformers.

Access to mobile phones in Africa has soared from 2 percent in 2000 to 39 percent by the end of 2009.[10] Excluding children under the age of 15, the "effective" penetration rate is already well over 50 percent in many countries.[11] Mobile telephony costs have also dropped steadily over the last decade. Increased competition among mobile operators prompted price reductions of 10-50 percent per call in many African countries in 2011.[12]

The rise in mobile telephony has been paralleled by the expansion of radio, which by comparison reaches many more Africans and has long been the continent's dominant mass media. According to Afrobarometer surveys, Africans still rely far more on radio than television or print media for news and information (see Table 2). This preference for radio has remained remarkably constant over the last 10 years, even as other forms of media, including mobile phones and the Internet, have grown.

While radio has been available in Africa for decades, until the opening of political space in the 1990s radio stations were limited in number, coverage, and typically controlled by the state. In 1988, the continent hosted just 10 independent radio stations.[13] Until the 2000s, many African countries still lacked a nationwide private radio station, meaning compatriots could not access the same independent media source. Some Africans simply had no exposure to independent mass media. However, between 2000 and 2006, commercial radio in Africa expanded by nearly 360 percent.[14] Community radio grew 1,386 percent. Hundreds of new stations have opened, connecting citizens within as well as across borders (see Figure 2).

Internet capacity across the continent is also expanding exponentially. In 2000, Africa was connected to its first undersea fiber optic cable. By 2009 two more were laid, providing a total of 2,580 gigabits/second of transmission capacity. By 2012, at least 12 newly laid cables will add an additional 31,640 gigabits/second of capacity, an increase of more than ten-fold in less than four years.[16]

This surge in internet connectivity is stimulating a rapid adoption of social media. In the last half of 2010, Africa emerged as the most dynamic continent on Facebook with growth rates surpassing Asia. Subscriber growth rates in 2011 in countries such as the Democratic Republic of the Congo (DRC) and Angola were over 50 percent (see Table 3). In Dakar, more than a third of the city has a Facebook profile. Nearly two thirds of all inhabitants in Accra have profiles — more than in San Antonio, Ottawa, or Hamburg.[17]

This multitrack expansion of independent media and information technologies in Africa has created unprecedented opportunities for public dialogue, debate, and empowerment.[19] It has considerably reduced the time and costs required to share information and is a major shift from the controlled one-directional information flows that have historically prevailed on the continent. By broadening access to information, the array of choices, options, and opportunities available to Africans has expanded. With the ability of farmers to find alternative markets for their crops, civil society organizations to independently tally election results, and citizens to send questions by text messages to talk radio shows during interviews of their political representatives, expectations are also changing.

The expansion of Information and Communication Technologies (ICTs) is also reshaping African citizens' ability to engage with one another and coordinate their actions. For example, widespread demonstrations and protests erupted in Mozambique in September 2010 following the circulation of text messages criticizing government responses to broad price increases. Many Mozambicans shared the sentiments of a 35-year-old protester who explained that "Even me, when I saw the message I forwarded it to other people. To my friends, my sister. 'I'm asking you, please read this message'."[20]   This mobilizing potential, however, is not without complications. Mass text messaging has also been used to feed intercommunal suspicions and violence in Nigeria, Kenya, and elsewhere.

Expanded radio coverage in Africa shares similarities with the growth and role of independent satellite television in the Arab world. The new medium provided a common forum where millions of viewers could learn and engage on issues that had long been considered off limits. As importantly, satellite TV helped create a shared consciousness of the challenges faced in Arab societies. This common forum has had an enormous educational and awareness-raising effect that, when combined with the personal communication and outreach potential of social media, have facilitated the mobilization of the general population in support of protest movements.

As a result of these changes, public priorities are now much more likely to be aired — as are requirements for governments to demonstrate responsiveness to these priorities. According to Afrobarometer surveys, respondents who are more connected to media also expressed a stronger interest in public affairs, reported that they more frequently discussed politics with friends and family, and were more likely to agree that opposition political parties should criticize the government.[21]

This impact is borne out in numerous examples from across Africa. In Kenya, citizens rated media as the most trusted source of information in the run-up to a national referendum on the new constitution in August 2010.[22] Though evidence of bias, unprofessional coverage, and sensationalism was found, an assessment of print, radio, television, online, and other Kenyan media coverage of the referendum concluded that media improved its role as informer, investigator, and forum for public debate compared to a national referendum in 2005 and presidential election in 2007. In the final days before the vote, many outlets repeatedly urged citizens to remain peaceful and "not to listen to the politicians but to choose from their own individual conscious."[23]

Following a military coup in Niger in early 2010, media became an important filter through which an institutional reform process engaged and communicated with the broader populace, contributing to a return to constitutional rule in 2011.[24] A study of interactive community radio programs in eastern DRC and the Central African Republic found that 86 percent of listeners reported an increased understanding of the role of their national authorities. Relative to previous years, 60 percent more listeners also reported accessing a local judicial authority in the previous three months.[25]

Mobile phones have become a critical source of information in Zimbabwe's heavily restricted media environment. Since its transmissions were blocked in many parts of the country, a foreign-based Zimbabwean online and radio news outfit created a subscription service to send news headlines via text message. Demand was so strong and rapid that the organization had to cap the number of subscribers due to the costs of sending tens of thousands of messages for each headline.[26] Similarly, a mobile phone-based news service called "Voice of Real Change" launched by Zimbabwe's opposition political party received 100,000 phone calls on its first day of operation in 2010.[27] The power of mobile telephony is not lost on the ruling party, which has sent mass text messages to Zimbabweans urging recipients to sign petitions to lift U.S. and European sanctions against the government.

In Uganda, voters were able to submit questions via Facebook during one of the final debates between mayoral candidates in Kampala in March 2011. The debate itself was streamed on television, radio, and the Internet. Coverage was also "live tweeted" by Ugandan independent media outlets.[28] The impact of real-time, widespread media coverage during Uganda's presidential elections in February was further reinforced when it emerged that the government was selectively blocking and monitoring SMS traffic that was referencing anti-government protests in Tunisia and Egypt.[29] After the election, large protests erupted when television footage of the violent arrest of opposition leader, Kizza Besigye, was captured by Ugandan media. Broadcasters were told to stop live coverage of the anti-government protests and many media companies encountered increased technical difficulties transmitting with web-based media, which was attributed to government interference.[30] More than anything Besigye could have said or done, the images capturing the government's heavy-handed response badly damaged the legitimacy of the Museveni regime, both domestically and internationally.

Facebook was also a potent tool in Nigeria's April 2011 presidential elections. Eventual winner President Goodluck Jonathan overcame several significant handicaps to his public image. At the beginning of the race he was viewed by many Nigerians as an insider of the ruling People's Democratic Party (PDP) who lacked vision and seemed subdued. By the time of his victory, many voters who disliked the PDP still voted for Jonathan, viewing him as a formidable interloper within the sclerotic ruling party. Much of this image makeover is attributable to his use of the Internet, specifically Facebook where he enjoys over 600,000 "likes" and is a regular user. President Jonathan has used Facebook to solicit feedback, conduct surveys, announce initiatives, and connect with Nigerians. His postings have elicited tens of thousands of comments.[31] By comparison, President Jonathan's main opponent Muhammadu Buhari has fewer than 20,000 followers on Facebook and launched his Internet campaign barely 6 weeks before election day.[32]

Despite these advances, many obstacles still inhibit the impact of mass media and information technology in Africa. Regulatory frameworks pose substantial hurdles. Senegal liberalized broadcast media in 2000, but only issued its first license to a private radio station in 2008.[33] Licensing in Nigeria has likewise been slow with legislation regarding community radio only becoming law in 2010.[34] Excessive and indiscriminate fees also raise the cost and predictability of funding a station.

Similar obstacles block new mobile and Internet companies from entering some African markets. Moreover, available credit and loans are few, management skills weak, and market research to facilitate advertising-based revenues extremely limited. The interest of some political actors to acquire media outlets to promote a particular ideological perspective, furthermore, can have polarizing and even destabilizing effects.

Nonetheless, the rapid growth of radio, mobile telephones, and the Internet is further testimony of a widespread desire among Africans for more and varied access to independent media. The depth and diversity of emerging information technologies as well as the importance of these tools to such broad swathes of Africans also make their growth difficult to reverse or control.

Deepening Civil Society

Civil society plays a critical role in a vibrant democracy. It facilitates public participation on issues of interest to the general population, allows citizens to take initiative to address local or national challenges rather than passively waiting for government to take action, and fosters independent ideas and solutions that enrich policy debates and contribute to better decision making. Civil society also plays an indispensible role in holding government actors accountable by serving as a watchdog over public budgeting, procurement practices, natural resource allocations, personnel appointments, the even-handed application of the rule of law, and the abuse of official power, among other facets of governance that are vulnerable to influence peddling or state capture. In all these ways, civil society serves as a vital check and balance in a democratic society.

More generally, civil society organizations help create social bonds across ethnic or geographic groups on matters of shared interest. In this way, civil society helps build and strengthen perceptions of national identity. This process is realized by the full range of civil society organizations — community groups, sports associations, cultural troupes, business associations, trade unions, social welfare agencies, as well as activists. That is, the process of citizens independently joining together to respond to some shared interest or social need also strengthens social bonds. This is in some ways as important as the primary object of their efforts. The manner in which civil society organizations are governed, in turn, serves as a valuable learning experience in democratic governance. To the degree that civil society organizations promote participation, transparency, cooperation, and the election and oversight of their own leaders, civil society groups help inculcate democratic values in a society.

Civil society is frequently stunted in societies that have long been dominated by autocratic governance structures. This was the case in most African countries with the inception of multiparty politics. Nonetheless, civil society organizations have typically been at the forefront of political reforms in Africa.[35] It was civil society that championed the historic national conferences of the early 1990s in West Africa that facilitated the initial transitions from autocratic rule. And with the greater openness of the past two decades, Africa's civil society organizations have grown in number, capacity, and sophistication. Today,

African civil society continues to campaign for anti-corruption initiatives, promote needed constitutional reforms, advocate for poverty alleviation, and oppose the prolongation of presidential terms.

This was vividly demonstrated even in long autocratic Guinea, where courageous civil society organizations led calls for greater openness during pro-democracy marches that eventually achieved a democratic breakthrough in 2010. Among other hardships they endured was a massacre of unarmed protesters at the national stadium in September 2009 by the then military government of Captain Dadis Camara in which up to 200 people were killed and hundreds more raped and injured. This event was pivotal in ramping up regional and international pressure on that regime.

While there is still great variance across countries in caliber and vibrancy, African civil society is a much more central feature of public life on the continent than it was 10 or 20 years ago. This is another important institutional difference in Africa from previous decades. The web of social organizations that creates an enabling environment for democracy to flourish is slowly being woven. Indeed, the strength of civil society and the social cohesion it fosters are vital factors in ensuring the resilience and sustainability of democratic reforms.

Emerging Institutional Checks and Balances

Africa's formal democratic structures were almost invariably weak during the initial democratic breakthroughs of the 1990s. However, the second decade of this reform process has seen a number of these institutions incrementally gain in capacity, influence, and independence. Given Africa's strong legacy of concentrated power in the executive branch, this progress is noteworthy. The combined effect is a growing array of constraints on executive power that did not previously exist.

Key among these has been the gradual emergence of Africa's legislatures. While legislatures have been progressively more represented by popularly elected legislators since the early 1990s, these bodies have only begun to assert greater autonomy in the past decade. Propelled by a new (though still minority) generation of politicians committed to reform, this change has been demonstrated by legislatures initiating and modifying a greater number of laws, reviewing and approving national budgets, and building legislative committee structures to enhance expert questioning of executive branch policies.[36] Nearly 60 percent of the bills introduced in the Kenya National Assembly in recent years, for example, are amended at either the committee or plenary stage.[37]

The growing role of the legislative branch in the national budgeting process is increasing the attention given to constituent priorities such as health and education.[38] Recognizing the popularity of these initiatives, legislative members have also become more active in ensuring development resources flow to their respective districts as part of their constituency services. The growing relevance of African legislatures to the policy process can be measured by the degree to which legislatures are being lobbied by civil society and business interests.[39]

African legislatures have also begun to play a more active oversight role of the executive branch by subpoenaing government officials and documents, as well as requiring progress reports of program implementation.[40] This is particularly important given the growing expectation that legislatures approve major aid packages (from the World Bank or Millennium Challenge Corporation, for example) as well as contracts with resource extraction firms. By creating a public platform for these issues of national interest, African legislatures are simultaneously raising awareness, heightening transparency of government contracting procedures, and increasing popular participation in the policymaking process.

Emblematic of this new assertiveness is the insistence of the Ugandan Parliament to review oil contracts the executive branch signed with the British oil extraction firm, Tullow Energy. These negotiations have been shrouded in secrecy ever since oil was discovered in Uganda in 2009. Increasingly concerned with high-level corruption, in October 2011 the Parliament slapped a ban on the execution of the contracts until the government explains its plans for operationalizing its oil and gas policy and accounts for all funds received from exploration.[41] Three ministers accused of accepting bribes during the contract negotiations were forced to step down pending a completion of the parliamentary investigation.

Legislatures have also been instrumental in blocking the repeal of term limits sought by a number of African heads of state, including in Malawi, Niger, Nigeria, and Zambia. Table 4 shows the degree to which the term limit issue has been at the center of the struggle to institute checks and balances on the executive branch in Africa over the past decade. Term limits have now been institutionalized in 15 African countries with stipulations in place in an additional 15 constitutions. While legislatures have not always been successful in upholding these limits (e.g. Cameroon, Chad, Djibouti, Gabon, Togo, and Uganda), the significant number of successes shows that the executive branch's monopolization of power in Africa is diminishing.

Legislators' focus on constituent interests is a function of the incentives they face to keep their positions. Proportional representation systems allocate seats in a legislature according to the percentage of votes won by respective political parties nationally. Legislative members are then selected based on their ranking on party-nominated candidate lists. Such arrangements reinforce legislators' allegiance to party leaders rather than the constituents in their home districts. Legislators who operate in lockstep, furthermore, are less likely to be champions of reform and oversight. In contrast, legislatures that are filled with candidates who win elections in their home jurisdictions have incentives to prioritize constituent interests.

While significant progress has been made, African legislatures for the most part continue to be constrained by limited salaries, budgets, staff, and expertise. This, in turn, makes them more susceptible to influential supporters who can bankroll their reelection campaigns. Likewise, while an increasing number of legislative sessions and hearings are open to the public, this is still an exception — missing an opportunity to build credibility with the general public while strengthening legislatures' role as a forum for public dialogue.

Africa's courts have also been incrementally growing more independent from executive branch control since the emergence of multipartyism on the continent. This has been seen most prominently in judgments on electoral rules that run counter to incumbent interests. Following the 2007 elections in Nigeria, for example, a dozen declared winners of state governorships from the ruling party had their elections annulled by the courts. During the same year, the Nigerian Supreme Court was instrumental in protecting the right of individual candidates to contest for National Assembly seats rather than leave this to the discretion of a powerful party leader or caucus, as had historically been the case. This principle was later formalized by the National Assembly in its 2010 Electoral Act.[43] Kenya's High Court similarly upheld the country's new constitution by requiring the president to vet nominations of key officials with the prime minister. This included appointments to such key roles as the Chief Justice, Attorney General, Director of Public Prosecutions, and the Budget Controller. In Niger, the constitutional court ruled three times that former President Mamadou Tandja's attempt to alter the constitution so that he could extend his time in power was illegal.

The increasing independence of the courts is a result of a combination of factors including more democratically elected political leaders nominating independent-minded judges based on their qualifications for the position, the growing practice of judicial nominations being vetted by parliamentary or special judicial oversight commissions, and the establishment of independent funds for paying judicial salaries that are outside the control of the executive branch.[44]

Paralleling the growing autonomy of African courts, Africa's Election Management Bodies (EMBs) have also been gaining traction in the wake of multipartyism. As elections are about choices between competing interests in a society, they are by nature contentious. A transparent, predictable, and level electoral playing field, therefore, is essential if stability is to be maintained and winning candidates gain the legitimacy that electoral events in democracies are intended to generate.

While there is a growing recognition of the importance of highly effective and credible EMBs, the process of creating them has been slow. In the 1990s the practice of presidents selecting electoral commissioners became a tool by which ruling parties could attempt to discretely influence electoral outcomes. Such tactics continue today, especially among the region's semi-authoritarian regimes. However, with the growing sophistication of electoral processes on the continent, including the increased involvement of international observers and parallel vote counts by civil society groups, bias within an EMB is increasingly conspicuous and self-defeating.

A key turning point in the recognition of the critical need for stronger EMBs in Africa came in 2007/2008. The run-up to a hotly contested presidential election on December 28, 2007 in Kenya had generated strong emotions that had become polarized along ethnic lines. Yet, bolstered by increasingly credible voting in 1997 and 2002, many assumed Kenya's 2007 elections would be managed effectively. Accordingly, relatively fewer international observers participated. In fact, the voting itself went smoothly — with 70 percent turnout. However, blatant ballot-stuffing during the vote-tallying ensued. Unexplained delays in the reporting of results generated a swirl of rumors and further escalated tensions. At nightfall three days later, the Electoral Commission of Kenya, members of which had been appointed by incumbent President Mwai Kibaki, announced that the president had won the election by a difference of 2 percentage points, and promptly certified the results. Kibaki was sworn in at a closed ceremony within hours. Destruction of most of the physical ballots before the official result was announced prevented any authoritative followup inquiry.

The announcement immediately set off clashes throughout Kenya leading to more than 1,500 deaths and the estimated displacement of 350,000 people. Occurring in one of Africa's most cosmopolitan societies, the Kenyan tragedy had broad reverberations around the continent. Indeed, many observers have argued that, despite the charged atmosphere and other shortcomings of the process, if Kenya's electoral commission had simply done its job and not certified elections until allegations of fraud were investigated, the violent aftermath could have been averted.

The distillation of this lesson was put into sharp relief with Ghana's electoral experience exactly one year later. In a tightly contended second-round presidential election, the opposition candidate, John Atta Mills, of the National Democratic Congress, eked out a victory — 50.2 to 49.8 percent — over the incumbent party candidate, Nana Akufo-Addo. Yet stability prevailed. Akufo-Addo publicly congratulated his rival and called on all Ghanaians to rally behind their new president.

Key to the successful outcome was the equanimity of Electoral Commission of Ghana (ECG). Despite enormous pressure to announce a result immediately following the close of the polls, the electoral commission waited five days for the votes from all jurisdictions to be counted and charges of irregularities investigated before certifying the results. The integrity of the process and the chairman of the ECG, Dr. Kwadwo Afari-Gyan, reassured the Ghanaian public that the outcome was fair. Empowered with this legitimacy, Atta Mills has subsequently overseen Ghana's continued rapid rate of economic growth.

The institutionalization of democracy in Africa can also be seen in the expanding role of local governments. Decentralization is commonly viewed as a means to enhance the degree of interface between a population and a government as well as improve incentives for responsiveness and accountability to local communities. This has practical advantages for countries with large populations or expansive geographic areas, allowing for the customized alignment of government services to local priorities. Strengthening local governments is also seen as a means to establish multiple poles of authority within a state — assuaging minority group fears of being dominated and fostering stability by enhancing a greater sense of local citizenship "ownership" or "buy-in" to their political system.

As with other democratic institution building in Africa, local government initiatives have gained more dynamism during the second decade since the reemergence of multipartyism. Today, nearly every African country holds some form of regularly scheduled local elections.[45] This has been accompanied by varying degrees of local political authority, access to fiscal resources, and especially administrative capacity. Countries that have made the strongest commitment to building local government authority, such as Tanzania, Uganda, and Ghana, have similarly benefitted from higher levels of state legitimacy.

The creation of this institutional architecture at the local level is a significant departure from the highly concentrated political systems that existed in the early 1990s. These local government offices, furthermore, have created more opportunities for citizen interactions with their governments. This is true even in political systems dominated by a single party.[46]

Still, for the most part, local government administrations in Africa remain relatively weak. Local government entities have tended to gain more autonomy in countries with competitive party systems. Where this is not the case, such as in Ethiopia and Burkina Faso, national party leaders have tended to exert considerable control, including over the lists of candidates that may compete for local office.[47]

This undercuts the incentive for accountability to local populations that local government structures are supposed to generate. Nonetheless, unlike the backsliding seen in other facets of democratization, there generally has not been a pattern of formal recentralization in Africa.[48]

In short, across a number of fronts, there is evidence of steadily expanding institutional checks and balances in many countries in Africa. The composite result is a meaningful departure from the reality of previous decades where there was a unipolar concentration of power in the executive branch, frequently in a single individual. Further reforms are required for the full benefits of these checks and balances to be realized. Nonetheless, the strengthening of these institutional structures is creating a stronger foundation for further democratic advances on the continent.

Rapid Urbanization and Youth Bulge

One of the biggest transformations underway in Africa is rapid urbanization. African cities are adding 15-18 million people each year. By 2025, it is estimated that more than half of Africa's population will live in urban areas — representing an unprecedented demographic reversal for the continent.[49] These changes are creating enormous strains on municipal governments as well as new threats to instability in the form of violent crime, gang activity, illicit trafficking, and links to transnational organized crime.

This demographic shift also has important political implications. Congregated populations have historically been relatively easier to inform and organize. This has facilitated political party formation and popular engagement with government. Urbanized populations can also be more readily mobilized for social or political protests — as vividly seen in Cairo and Tunis. Relying as they do on cash income and markets to meet basic needs, rather than their farms, urban dwellers are also much more vulnerable to fluctuations in prices. Accordingly, cities have been the locus of riots resulting from food and other basic shortages in Burkina Faso, Cameroon, Malawi, Mauritania, Mozambique, Senegal, and South Africa, among others, in recent years.

With 70 percent of the total population under 30 years of age, Africa is the world's youngest continent.[50] This creates a vitality and dynamism conducive to change. Youth are typically the vanguard of reform for a society — less willing to accept persistent inequities and the misuse of power. This is particularly true of this generation, which is the most educated in Africa's history with average primary school enrollment having increased from 59 percent in 1999 to 77 percent in 2009 (see Figure 3). Similar gains have been realized in secondary and tertiary enrolment levels. Moreover, youth are leading the embrace of mobile phones and information technology on the continent. This has made them better informed and more aware of living conditions and governance standards elsewhere in Africa and the world — an awareness that is reshaping expectations youth have of their own governments. All these factors are positive forces for change in Africa compared to even a decade ago.

Africa's youth are also a potent economic force, comprising 37 percent of the workforce. This is reflective of a growing African middle class estimated at 85 million households — a figure that is expected to double in the next 10 years.[52] Nonetheless, youth unemployment is a concern. As a whole, the region faces a 12 percent youth unemployment rate, though this varies greatly across countries. Youth unemployment is less than 5 percent in Malawi and Rwanda, whereas it surpasses 20 percent in Ghana, Zambia, and Zimbabwe, and is above 30 percent in Botswana, Lesotho, Mauritius, Namibia, Swaziland, and South Africa.[53] There is also a high degree of underemployment and working poverty. This reflects the limited job opportunities in the public sector as well as constraints on obtaining credit, land, and licenses that would enable entrepreneurs to start businesses. Combined, these factors are fueling greater frustration with the status quo among Africa's youth — and higher demands on governments to deliver.

Rising Regional and International Standards

Another important change to the democratization landscape in Africa is the shift in governance norms endorsed by regional bodies. This was reflected in the Constitutive Act of the AU in 2002, which emphasized the principles of good governance, popular participation, the rule of law, and human rights. Drawing from this, the AU adopted the African Charter on Democracy, Elections, and Governance in 2007 — essentially an aspirational statement of governance values and principles for the continent. Since then there have been growing expectations that the AU and Africa's Regional Economic Communities (RECs) should actively narrow the gap between this aspiration and reality. This has resulted in incremental though steadily greater engagement to condemn and reverse unconstitutional changes in power. This was evident in the insistence by ECOWAS that the November 2010 electoral outcome in Côte d'Ivoire be upheld, their criticism of Nigerien President Mamadou Tandja's attempt to prolong his hold on power through unconstitutional means in 2009, the imposition of arms embargoes and sanctions against the Guinean military's coup leaders, constructive engagement with the Nigerien and Guinean militaries for a transition back to civilian rule, and refusing to recognize the attempted installation of Faure Gnassingbé as president of Togo by the military following the death of his father, Gnassingbé Eyadéma, in 2005.[54]

ECOWAS has been the leading regional actor in promoting constitutionally based transfers of power. This is a principle borne from the fire of instability generated by a spate of civil wars that engulfed West Africa starting in the early 1990s. In addition to the above cases, ECOWAS was actively involved in democratic transitions in Sierra Leone and Liberia. It also regularly and proactively deploys members of its Council of the Wise, its Mediation and Security Council, and regional police personnel to defuse political crises and monitor elections in the subregion. This has all helped raise the bar that political authorities in West Africa must meet in order to be recognized as legitimate. This commitment has made West Africa a locus of democratic reform. Currently, only three of ECOWAS's 15 heads of state have been in power for more than 10 years. Moreover, as new democratically elected leaders come into office, they are further shifting the standards and priorities of this subregional body.

A novel though still nascent feature of Africa's efforts to elevate its governance standards has been the introduction of the African Peer Review Mechanism (APRM). Rooted in African values of individual responsibility to the collective, this process requires a participating African government to undergo a periodic review of its political, economic, corporate governance, and security values and standards by its African peers. To date, 30 countries have signed on to the process and 14 have been peer reviewed. This process results in a formal report to the respective government, which is then able to respond — generating new opportunities for public discourse and oversight. While the APRM has not progressed as far or as fast as many had hoped, the process is reinforcing regional norms for democracy as virtually every participating government extols its democratic credentials as a basis for its claims on authority.

Despite this progress in advancing democratic norms on the continent, it is important to recognize a growing divergence in support for these principles among regional bodies. In particular, the AU has not generally been at the forefront of recent democratic breakthroughs. The AU was surprised by and unable to organize a common position toward the popular uprisings in Egypt and Tunisia. Subsequently, it was awkwardly late in recognizing Libya's National Transitional Council (NTC) relative to virtually every other relevant international organization. The AU has thus positioned itself as being less supportive of democratic change than the Arab League. In fact the AU was out of step with its own membership with 22 African states recognizing the NTC before the AU finally did. A similar, though less stark, pattern emerged in the postelection standoff in Côte d'Ivoire. Whereas ECOWAS took an early and decisive stand in support of the election outcome, the AU position was more equivocal. In addition, the AU negotiation team was seen by many to be operating on a parallel track to the ECOWAS efforts. The effect was to diminish the strong subregional and international consensus to uphold democratic principles, providing Laurent Gbagbo more room to claim regional support for his position. In this and other recent cases, furthermore, some of the AU representatives selected to engage in the crises did not themselves have strong democratic credentials. In short, the AU's laggardly leadership on these transitions has created fresh questions over its commitment to the democratic values it espouses.

The issue is of importance since experience from Africa and other regions has shown that democratic norms exert a gravitational pull. As the median level of democracy in a region rises, it elevates the degree of democracy realized in each respective state beyond what it would have been otherwise. This pattern attests to the power of "demonstration effects." Citizens in one nation replicate and expect the same positive developments they observe unfolding among their neighbors. It is partly for this reason that democratic changes tend to occur in clusters. Such a phenomenon has clearly been at play in the sequential unfolding of protests across North Africa and the Middle East once the vision of change took hold in Tunisia.

The shift in regional democratic norms has been matched by heightened standards internationally. After decades of being an off-limits issue in international discourse, regime orientation has become a much more central and defining feature in relations between states. To a large extent this reflects the seismic shift in global governance patterns of the past two decades. In the late 1980s, roughly one-third of the world's states were democratic-leaning. Today, with the end of the Cold War, some two-thirds of the world's states are on a democratic path. Democratic swings in Eastern Europe and Latin America generated a wealth of knowledge on how such transitions occur and the challenges they face. They also spurred the development of institutional and technical expertise for democracy assistance among international donors.

Long a dominant actor in Africa given its colonial legacy, France is undergoing a change in its policy towards autocratic governments on the continent. For most of the post-colonial period, France has maintained a clear realpolitik policy in Africa. Close ties and fidelity to French interests have greatly outweighed legitimacy considerations. In fact, France has a long track record of militarily intervening to support friendly autocratic leaders in Africa who would otherwise have been toppled. With the accession of President Nicolas Sarkozy in 2007, this approach has started to change. France has adopted a policy of "non-interference," signaling that it would no longer come to the rescue of its (autocratic) allies in Africa and instead would broaden relations with Africa's democracies. Sarkozy has gone so far as to say, "…all those who are persecuted by tyrannies and dictatorships…could count on France."[55] This may be part of a broader shift in French views of Africa, as demonstrated by a November 2010 French high court ruling authorizing an investigation of the assets held by three African dictators and their family members.[56] While many argue that France's policy in Africa is still dominated by expediency, France plays a more constructive role in democratic development than at any other point in the postcolonial era.

The shift in global democracy patterns is, in turn, shaping the positions and actions of multilateral institutions. The United Nations (UN) under Secretary General Kofi Annan began talking much more openly about states adhering to democratic practices. A UN Democracy Caucus was established in 2004 and the UN Democracy Fund, aimed at supporting democratization around the world, was created the following year. Making democracy a criterion for accession to the European Union was a powerful incentive for numerous former Eastern Bloc countries to persist in their democratization efforts. Similarly, adhering to basic democratic norms has been a central feature of the coalition of Commonwealth countries and the trade, aid, and reputational benefits membership therein affords. The Commonwealth has upheld the integrity of these standards by at times suspending members, such as Zimbabwe and Nigeria, for poor governance. And belonging to such multinational groupings has cachet, as evidenced by applications submitted for Commonwealth membership by countries without constitutional links to the United Kingdom, such as Algeria, Madagascar, Mozambique, and Rwanda (of which the latter two are now members).

A number of bilateral donor agencies, most prominently the United States' Millennium Challenge Corporation, have begun taking democracy explicitly into consideration when disbursing aid. Similarly, donors are much more likely than in the past to withhold or cease aid when a heretofore democratic government stops governing in a democratic manner, as was seen with the cessation of payments to Malawi following the lethal crackdown on protesters in July 2011. Likewise, donors held back disbursements to Kenya because of concerns over corruption and the indictment by the International Criminal Court (ICC) of leading politicians for their alleged role in the postelection violence of 2007/2008.

Accompanying these shifting patterns of governance norms has been a growing sense of international responsibility to respond to security and humanitarian crises, even when such intervention is opposed by the state in which the crisis is unfolding. This principle was crystallized in the UN Resolution on the "Responsibility to Protect" adopted in 2009. This statement reflects a substantial evolution in the interpretation of sovereignty and governance norms from a few decades earlier when state sovereignty was sacrosanct. Today, emphasis on citizen sovereignty is increasingly prevalent.

This evolution in international consciousness, coupled with the end of Cold War rivalries in Africa, led to an upsurge in international engagement to mitigate conflict on the continent. Since 2000, there have been 40 UN- or AU-sanctioned peace operations in Africa.[57] This includes 13 UN peacekeeping operations, which are widely considered to have contributed to the steady decline in the number of conflicts on the continent.

In short, regional and international policy has historically had a significant influence on Africa's governance norms — be it through the colonial, Cold War, or post-Cold War eras. The heightened centrality democratic governance plays in regional and international relations today will likely further encourage emerging democratic values in Africa.

Countervailing Forces

While there are a number of institutional drivers advancing democracy in Africa, the horizon is far from clear. Rather, the course forward is complicated by various forces resistant to change that must also be considered. Sustaining and advancing democratic progress in Africa will require overcoming, or at least neutralizing, these obstacles.

Weak sense of national identity. Many African countries are still in a process of nation-building. While there is considerable variance between and within societies, individuals often continue to identify more with one's ethnic group or clan than with one's nationality.[58] These divisions have been perpetuated by the defining role ethnicity has played in exclusive (often minority-based) governance coalitions in numerous countries. Given the winner-take-all nature of many systems where political power is closely associated with economic opportunity and social advancement, these arrangements have generated deep resentments within numerous African societies. It has also fostered a determination by excluded groups to orchestrate outcomes where they will have "their turn" to control the spigots of state revenues. Such a divisive organizing dynamic works against building the social cohesion and trust needed to sustain legitimate governance structures and equity-based development.

Africa's rapid urbanization and the broader international exposure afforded by modern communications may be eroding the pull of ethnicity, while strengthening national identity. Indeed, this change in perspective has been seen in some urban areas in Africa, particularly among youth. However, the effectiveness with which politicians can continue to mobilize populations along ethnic lines, as seen in relatively cosmopolitan Nairobi following the disputed 2007 elections, suggests that the nation-building process is still a work in progress.

Limited civil society. Despite its noteworthy gains, the strength of civil society varies greatly across Africa. In many countries, civil society is weak and fragmented, engaging only a sliver of the population, mainly in urban areas.[59] Civil society under such conditions is susceptible to cooption by a governing regime which can offer financial assistance and privileged access to compliant organizations. Moreover, rather than building bonds across society along issues of shared interest, civil society groups are frequently organized along intergroup differences, reinforcing societal divisions. Similarly, too often, these civil society groups are highly personality driven — at times serving the political interests of an individual rather than a broader social concern. Not coincidentally, these organizations are often governed with the same limitations on participation, expression, free and fair leadership elections, and accountability as a governing regime, making them poor training grounds for democratic models of governance.

Neopatrimonial legacies. Nearly every African society has been shaped by neopatrimonial or "big-man" governance models that reinforce notions that executives not only make but are above the law. As a result, government systems revolve around the interests of the individual at the expense of the general public. The result is that state institutions, especially accountability structures, remain weak. Overcoming these legacies is at the heart of the democratization challenge in Africa. The issue is particularly problematic in that this model remains strong even in some of Africa's more advanced democracies and democratizers such as Senegal, Malawi, and Benin — and account for the backsliding observed there. It also dovetails with the persistence of semi-authoritarian governance models in Africa. These systems have adopted some of the instruments of democracy, though because of the prevalence of the neopatrimonial culture and weak institutions, power remains largely monopolized by the executive. The model is particularly pernicious since it projects an impression of democracy — though with none of the benefits. It thus simultaneously confounds what democracy requires while fostering disillusion over what it can deliver relative to previous autocratic models. Moreover, to the extent regional and international actors deem semi-authoritarian leaders legitimate, it solidifies a low standard of political reform. Incentives for further change and genuine democratization are minimal.

Weak political parties. Closely related to neopatrimonial legacies and the stunting of political institutions that have resulted is the feeble state of African political parties. Not dissimilar from the regimes they seek to replace, opposition parties are often personality rather than issues based. They, therefore, are less rooted at the local level and struggle to mobilize the broad popular participation needed to win elections and sustain reform. Indeed, their individualistic focus is why so many of Africa's opposition parties are unable to come together in a coalition to unseat an unpopular incumbent. In the same way, many African political parties fail to brand themselves by a single governing philosophy or set of policies that remain consistent from election to election. Accordingly, there is little incentive for sustained loyalty and funding support among a broad base of citizens committed to shared ideals. Rather, African political parties are constantly reinventing themselves — and, as such, reintroducing themselves to a skeptical public. Ethnically based overtones, common to many of these parties, minimize opportunities to build crosscutting constituencies.

Politicized security sectors. Another common feature of Africa's neopatrimonial political model is the politicization of the security sector. To be more precise, this commonly entails the politicization of the presidential guard (or special elite force responsible for the protection of the president) that often belongs primarily to the same ethnic group as the head of state. These units are typically outsized for their role and are disproportionately compensated and equipped relative to other elements of the security sector. Accordingly, the loyalties of these units are with the head of state rather than the institutions of the state. This incentive structure is by design and is a key factor perpetuating personalistic governance models and weak professionalism in the security sector. The operational mandate of these politicized forces is regime protection rather than citizen protection. The persistence of such forces are further obstacles to enhancing legitimacy in Africa.

Natural resource curse. Over fifty percent of Africa's autocracies and semi-authoritarians are considered natural resource rich.[60] These revenues enable these regimes to sustain the patronage networks and coercive capacity needed to maintain their hold on power far beyond what they would otherwise be capable. Considerable empirical evidence shows that abundant natural resource revenues flowing into an unaccountable governance context accelerates corruption, inequality, economic distortions that stymie development, and instability. Access to these outsized revenues also renders these governments less receptive to aid and trade incentives for reform.

China. While China has expanded its economic presence throughout the continent in the past decade, it has often focused its engagement on the region's autocratic and poorly governed states (e.g. Zimbabwe, Sudan, Guinea, and Angola). This has resulted in budget transfers, at times to the tune of several billion dollars, to regimes that would otherwise face internal and external pressure for governance reform. China has also been a major arms supplier to these regimes, sometimes in violation of United Nations sanctions. Moreover, China has actively promoted a return to the principle of state sovereignty or "noninterference" as part of its engagement approach on the continent. Unsurprisingly, this concept is very popular with Africa's autocrats who would welcome a reversion to an era of impunity for human rights abuses and humanitarian catastrophe. China has also presented itself as offering an alternate governance model to the emerging democratic norms on the continent. The notion that autocracies can deliver rapid development and stability, while refuted by a long track record of disastrous autocratic performance on the continent, provides a popular platform from which Africa's political leaders can justify their extended tenures in power.

Fallout from Libya. Libyan leader Colonel Muammar Gaddafi long played a destabilizing role in Africa. He created an "Islamic Legion," mainly comprised of immigrants from Chad, Tunisia, Algeria, Niger, Mali, and Guinea to advance his goal of Arabizing the region. He subsequently dispatched legionnaires to Uganda, Chad, Mali, and Niger.[61] Some of these fighters later became Janjaweed leaders instrumental in the genocide in Darfur. He also used armed mercenaries from throughout the Sahel to bolster his security forces — which one Tuareg leader in Mali estimated amounted to some 16,000 fighters in early 2011.[62] In an effort to expand his influence in Africa, Gaddafi provided training for presidential protection units and weapons to many parts of West Africa. One illustration of this was the training and sponsoring of Charles Taylor and Foday Sankoh and their instigation of more than a decade of turmoil in Liberia, Sierra Leone, and the surrounding region.

The downfall of the Gaddafi regime and the cessation of these destabilizing activities will surely be positive for Africa. However, tens of thousands of African migrant workers, perhaps more, who had been sending remittances to their home countries, have lost their incomes. Moreover, Libyan businesses and finance institutions closely aligned with the Gaddafi regime had invested billions of dollars in hotels, banks, petrol stations, media enterprises, construction projects, large agricultural schemes, and other initiatives in numerous African countries including Zimbabwe, Sudan, Chad, Niger, Mali, Mauritania, the Central African Republic, Burkina Faso, Gabon, Uganda, and Kenya, among others.[63] Libya has also been a leading funder of the AU, accounting for roughly 15 percent of its total annual operating budget. The rapid drawdown of Libyan assets, accordingly, may destabilize certain African economies. Likewise, the flow of unsecured arms and mercenaries from Libya could spark greater and extended instability in a number of African countries, particularly Chad, Mali, Mauritania, Niger, Sudan, and Guinea.

This review has highlighted the breadth of dynamism underway in Africa. Many vital factors shaping key governance principles and institutions in Africa are shifting. Translating these trends into genuine democratic change, however, must overcome entrenched interests and significant counter-pressures. Africa's governance seas, accordingly, are rough with crosscurrents. The ultimate outcome these contending influences will have on Africa's democratic course remains to be seen.

Prospects For Democratic Transitions

To gain better perspective on how these competing trends will play out, it will be helpful to review some of the key mechanisms that have facilitated democratic change historically. Given the qualitative, contextual, and ultimately unique elements of each transition, one must use caution in applying hard-and-fast formulas to predict democratic transitions. Nonetheless, some drivers for change hold more currency among democracy scholars and provide a framework from which to examine Africa's current democratization prospects.

Elections. While it may seem so obvious as to not merit mentioning, democratic change occurs through elections resulting in a shift toward a more reformist leadership. This has been the case even in contexts where elections were not free and fair. Perhaps the most famous example was the defeat of Serbian strongman Slobodan Milošević in the 2002 elections that he had heavily tilted to his advantage. Even so, young democracy activists were able to use the occasion to organize the general population, make the elections competitive, ensure there was a parallel vote count, expose the hollow support for the ruling party, and ultimately defeat his brutal regime in a nonviolent, electoral process.

Even rigged elections can generate change as a regime risks exposing its illegitimacy by the extent to which it seeks to manipulate the process. This injustice, in turn, can spark the outrage that mobilizes the mass protests that can pressure an autocratic leader to step down. Such was the case when Ukrainian Prime Minister Viktor Yanukovych attempted to claim victory even though he had badly lost the 2004 presidential elections. The perceived injustice set off the Orange Revolution that eventually led to Viktor Yushchenko taking power , ushering in a period of democratic change in Ukraine. Similarly, it was Laurent Gbagbo's attempt to misrepresent and stonewall his electoral loss that led to his eventual removal from power. Likewise, deeply flawed electoral processes in Kenya in 2007 and Zimbabwe in 2008 badly discredited the legitimacy of the incumbents in both cases (though each was able to retain significant authority through ad hoc power-sharing agreements with the rightful victors).

Africa's democratic prospects are improving, then, if for no other reason than that elections are increasingly regular and numerous. With 14 presidential and 30 parliamentary elections as well as 3 national referenda slated between mid-2011 and the end of 2012 (see Table 5), there are, on average,

2 to 3 national elections being held on the continent every month. Of the presidential elections, 30 percent will not have an incumbent running, significantly increasing the likelihood that opposition parties may come to power.[65] Even incumbents' reelections are becoming less automatic. This was the case in September 2011, when longtime opposition candidate Michael Sata defeated incumbent Rupiah Banda in Zambia. Whereas one could previously count the number of African leaders replaced through elections on a single hand, this is no longer the case. While not yet the norm, alternations of power through elections are becoming more common in Africa. Thus, the perceived need for opposition groups to resort to violence to gain power is reduced. Likewise, these electoral events will serve as focal points for democracy proponents to challenge and place a spotlight on illegitimate regimes.

Meanwhile, the process of stealing elections is becoming more difficult in Africa. In order for an election to meet the legitimacy standard, there is a growing expectation that independent national and international electoral observers must be present and that civil society be involved in monitoring the vote count. The now ubiquitous presence of mobile phone video cameras that can capture and disseminate irregularities in a matter of minutes also means that rigging and manipulation are much harder to conceal. Indeed, the growing presence of mobile phones has been cited as a reason why Nigeria's April 2011 presidential election went as smoothly as it did.[66] In short, incumbent regimes are being forced into higher standards of accountability, often against their will.

Electoral violence remains a key concern for Africa's democratization experience with high-profile episodes in Kenya, Zimbabwe, and Nigeria in recent years reinforcing this image. Fed by politicians mobilizing supporters on an "us vs. them" platform, these clashes have broken out along ethnic lines in the days following elections. They have been further fueled by antagonistic messages circulated via media outlets aligned with a particular party or candidate. While these threats are real and must be addressed, they overshadow the growing regularity of peaceful elections on the continent.

Economic stagnation. Historical experience has shown that democratic breakthroughs are much more likely in contexts experiencing slow or contracting economic growth.[67] Often this exposes the gross mismanagement of the economy by autocratic rulers who leave power in the midst of economic crisis, handicapping the early years of a new democratic regime. Such periods of decline are also more likely to expose inequities that have been shaped by political monopolies tied to corruption and exclusive patronage networks. It is, therefore, an explosive context in which riots over access to food, jobs, and fuel are more likely.

Figure 4 shows the strong relationship between corruption and stagnant growth. African countries with weaker controls on corruption were much more likely to have experienced stagnant or contracting economic growth over the previous five years. Zimbabwe, Chad, Comoros, Guinea, Côte d'Ivoire, Madagascar, Guinea-Bissau, Burundi, the Democratic Republic of the Congo, and Togo all fall in the lower left "high corruption & stagnant growth" quadrant. Countries with above average controls on corruption, in contrast, tended to realize eight-fold greater gains in per capita income during the previous five years.

Notably since 2000, autocratic governments in Africa have typically generated economic performance that is 40 percent slower than that of democracies (even slower when oil revenues are excluded). Slow growth removes a key pillar rationalizing autocratic governance — that they are more effective (what some have called "performance legitimacy") and provide greater stability at the early stages of the development process. Lacking this claim of effectiveness, a regime's illegitimacy becomes more apparent and untenable.

Perhaps more importantly for social instability is that autocratically governed societies perform relatively more poorly, on average, across a whole host of social welfare measurements.[69] This reflects an inability to translate economic growth into tangible benefits for a majority of a population. Egypt and Tunisia, for example, had realized steady economic growth over the past several decades. However, growing disparities in levels of well being contributed to the broad-based angst that fueled the uprisings in both countries.

In Africa, 10 countries stand out for their particularly poor development performance (see Table 6). Using progress in reducing infant mortality rates over the past decade as a broad indicator of development, these countries have had higher than median levels of underperformance even though they have had better than average levels of per capita income for the region. This suggests that their governments have been less able or willing to mobilize the resources at their disposal to address societies' pressing social needs. Anger and resentment in these contexts are likely particularly acute. Indeed, this issue was a major factor in mobilizing support against Laurent Gbagbo in Côte d'Ivoire. Notably, eight of the nine others are autocracies. While not on the list because of their lower than median incomes, Chad and the Democratic Republic of the Congo also stand out for having regressed or made virtually no progress in reducing their infant mortality rates over the past decade. The lagging performance of the sole democracy on the list, São Tomé and Príncipe, is also a point of concern and priority for redress lest democratic gains there be set back.

Economic growth in autocracies is also much more subject to sharp fluctuations — on average, twice as volatile as growth in democracies.[70] Inflation, a result of monetary mismanagement, also tends to be higher. Inflation, consequently, creates enormous strains on ordinary citizens who, already living hand to mouth, do not have a buffer to weather even a 10 percent loss in value of their incomes. Accordingly, periods of economic downturn and instability, characteristic of autocratic settings, create regular stressor points for these regimes to stay in power.

While less subject to volatility and more resilient overall, periods of economic decline also present risks for democratizers. In fact, over 70 percent of all democratic backsliding occurs in situations of economic stagnation. Economic stress, therefore, should be monitored for its impact on Africa's ability to maintain positive democratic momentum.

Fracturing support for ruling regime. Another common feature that characterizes autocratic regime change is the loss of support from key constituents for regime leaders. "Constituents" from an autocratic perspective typically means the security sector, the ruling political party, key tribal leaders, patronage networks, and a quorum of business interests. "Defections" from these core groups toward a reform movement are instrumental in forcing a regime to accept power-sharing or precipitate the fall of the regime altogether.

Perhaps most critical of these constituents is the security sector. It provides the coercive capacity to intimidate the population into compliance and repress any organized effort to challenge regime authority. Without this coercive capacity an autocratic system is unable to sustain its hold on power. Recognizing this, former Tunisian President Zine El Abidine Ben Ali quickly fled the country once the Tunisian military refused to open fire on protesters. Likewise, the Egyptian military's recognition that citizens' right to protest was protected under the constitution and that it would not use violence against protesters was a turning point in the fall of the Mubarak regime.

This dynamic underscores that the professionalization of the security sector is a critical step in the democratization process.[71] The degree to which the security sector is committed to protecting the institutions of the state versus the interests of the regime, the less autocratic leaders will be able to sustain their hold on power. This is why autocracies make a point of undermining this professionalism and instead cultivate personal loyalty from security leaders — through ethnic ties, higher salaries, and privileged status relative to other security personnel.

Maintaining the support of patronage networks also requires ongoing effort and attention by regime leaders as the expectations of these networks expand over time. This "inflation of corruption" places ever greater pressure on regime leaders to divert state revenues to maintain this support.[72] Reliable access to these revenues depends on a healthy economy, which becomes more difficult to achieve the more substantial the distorting effects of the patronage arrangements. In addition to time in power, the pace of this inflation is a function of the degree of illegitimacy of a regime. Less legitimate regimes rely more heavily on their patronage networks, which can thus demand more for their support. Regimes that have been in power for a longer time may have higher burdens in this regard. Since aging leaders may have less credibility with which to sustain their support networks, their vulnerability to defections increases.[73]

Table 7 shows the propensity for poor performance among leaders who have been in power for prolonged durations. Several patterns stand out. First, Africa continues to have a large number of leaders who have been in place for a long time. Nineteen heads of state have held this role for 10 years or more. Eleven leaders are into their third decade of power. The flipside of this is that a spate of successions can be expected in the near future. Next, as one might expect, nearly all of the leaders who have been in place for more than a decade are autocracies, the exceptions being Cape Verde, Lesotho, and Senegal. Aside from these three, two-thirds of these states score below the African median on corruption perception. Likewise, save for those with natural resource revenues, many of these autocracies have experienced stagnant economic growth during the past five years. Seventy percent underperform on infant mortality, a proxy for broader development. In short, the longer leaders stay in power, the more likely their populations bear the cost.

Cohesion of reform movement. Beyond structural factors or preexisting conditions, the organizational sophistication and unity of a reform movement are decisive factors in fostering transitions from autocratic rule.[74] The logic of this rationale is that democratic reformers represent the interests of the majority of citizens who do not benefit from exclusive governance arrangements. As per the classic collective action challenge, however, the impediments to coordinating this majority keeps them disempowered relative to the smaller, better informed, better organized minority who control the levers of state power. The skills, vision, organizing capacity, and discipline of reform networks to raise awareness, mobilize, and sustain engagement of this majority against certain pushback, therefore, is decisive.

A 2005 study by Freedom House that evaluated 67 democratic transitions around the world over the previous 3 decades found that 50 were civil society based "bottom-up" initiatives involving strikes, boycotts, civil disobedience, and mass protests.[75] Key to this effort is building broadly representative coalitions of civic groups that are unified around strategic objectives, well organized, and disciplined in the use of nonviolence.

The use of nonviolence is particularly important. It facilitates the participation of a wider swath of the population, including the middle class, who may be willing to join a boycott or protest but are not interested in shooting anyone. Likewise, refraining from the use of violence denies a rationale for the regime to assert its dominant advantage in the use of force. Nonviolent tactics have also been shown to be most effective for peeling off support from the regime, particularly from the security sector, which is less willing to fire on unarmed protesters than to return fire on combatants.[76]

Strategies of civil resistance are often incremental but their effects cumulative.[77] Small successes can be translated into larger undertakings. Change rarely comes quickly, though. Calls for reform are likely to be met with strong resistance from the regime. This is why spontaneous protests rarely generate meaningful transformation. Rather the capacity for planning, organizing, and adapting to the challenges of the local context is what is needed. Civic organizations' ability to sustain momentum is indispensible for gaining traction, expanding the number of supporters, and appealing to regime constituents. The cohesiveness of civil society, especially the reform coalition, is a strong predictor of its ability to sustain these efforts in the face of resistance and realize successful democratization.[78]

Implications for Africa's Democratic Trajectory

Previous sections have reviewed a number of the key influences reshaping Africa's governance landscape. Taken together, what implications does this confluence of factors have for African democracy moving forward? Table 8 provides a compilation of some of the principal drivers influencing the movement toward (or backsliding from) democracy for each Sub-Saharan African country, organized by current regime classification. As the empirics behind the degree to which individual factors cause a shift toward democratization remain imprecise, this chart is intended to be descriptive rather than predictive. Nonetheless, the compilation allows certain patterns and insights to be discerned.

An immediate observation is the significantly different complexions of the respective regime categories. Countries rated as consolidating democracies tend to be pursuing policies that are enhancing democratic practices as reflected by the preponderance of top-tier (green shaded) scores realized in this category. A gradation of scores can be seen from this group through to the autocratic category, in which factors inhibiting democratic development (red shaded scores) dominate. This holds, in general, not only for the politically oriented factors (e.g. leader duration in office, depth of civil society, degree of media freedom) but also for the economic influences on democracy (economic growth, development progress, corruption, oil wealth, and inflation). At the same time, there is considerable variance within each regime category and within the scores for individual countries, reflecting the competing forces influencing the evolution of democracy on the continent, and cautioning against sweeping generalizations.

Nearly all of the countries in the consolidating democracies category benefit from active civil societies and leaders who have been in power for less than a decade. (The lone exception is Cape Verde where the prime minister has held this post for 11 years and recently won a third term). Still, mediocre performances on a number of these drivers underscore the incompleteness of the democratization process in most of these countries. This is evident in the limitations on media freedom and Internet access seen in Benin and Botswana, for example. Africa's leading democracies have also benefited from not having had to navigate the potentially corrupting influence of substantial oil revenues. However, oil revenues expected to come online in the coming years in Ghana will place additional strains on this government. Both Ghana and São Tomé and Príncipe are also facing the potentially destabilizing effects of high levels of inflation.

Consistent with patterns seen globally, economic growth rates among Africa's consolidating democracies are not exceptional — but they are steady and therefore stabilizing. Moreover, they do excel, by and large, in their development progress. The most vulnerable of these consolidating democracies would appear to be São Tomé and Príncipe with exceptionally slow developmental progress, high inflation, and only medium controls over corruption. Its relatively long duration in the democratic camp should serve as a bulwark against systematic backsliding, though.

Including as it does countries that have just started down a democratic path as well as those that have been establishing their democratic credentials for some time, the democratizer category reflects a wide spectrum of progress. Most positively for the forward momentum of this group is that leaders in 17 of 19 of these countries have been in power for less than a decade. This reflects the growing frequency of elections to select and replace leaders. Of the two exceptions (Lesotho and Senegal), Abdoulaye Wade of Senegal has come under increasing resistance to his efforts to seek another term. This group of democratizers also benefits from not relying on oil revenues — and the distorting political and economic effects this has. Only one country in this category, Nigeria, is considered "oil rich" and it has been making notable progress in opening its democratic institutions in the decade since it broke away from its military-led governance model. By maintaining recent advances, other candidate countries for transitioning into the democracy category include Kenya, Namibia, the Seychelles, Sierra Leone, and Zambia.

Still, this group of democratizers faces many challenges to consolidating their democratic institutions. Notably, none have attained the status of "free" in Freedom House's annual survey of press freedom — and two, Burundi and Madagascar, are considered to have sufficient media restrictions to fall into the "not free" delineation. A similar pattern, by and large, holds with regards to Internet access. Only Kenya, Nigeria, and the Seychelles distinguish themselves in this area.

The chart also highlights the strains facing a number of these democratizers. Young democratizers, Côte d'Ivoire and especially Guinea, must overcome the legacy of stagnant economic growth, corruption, and high inflation (including the trebling of the size of the armed forces in both countries over the past decade) they have inherited from their autocratic predecessors. The high propensity of backsliding in the early years of a democratic transition noted earlier in this report, therefore, is clearly at play here. The scores also point to the tenuous hold that a number of these democratizers, especially Burundi, Comoros, Guinea-Bissau, and Madagascar have in maintaining their democratic progress.

Within the semi-authoritarian category, the effect of entrenched leadership becomes sharply apparent. Seven of the 10 countries in this category have had leaders in place for 10 years or more. Moreover, there are tight restrictions on civil society and media freedom in most of these contexts. Interestingly, though, there is relatively more openness with regards to Internet access — with 7 of the 10 allowing median levels of access or better. Also noteworthy among this category is the relatively low reliance on oil revenues. Only the DRC and Gabon are considered oil rich. Given they have fewer resources with which to buttress patronage networks, it is perhaps not coincidental that only a minority of these regimes are perceived as among the most corrupt on the continent. This combination of a modicum of information access, limits on natural revenue largess, and medium levels of corruption suggests there is some degree of malleability in these governance structures towards greater levels of openness.

Key candidates for moving into the democratizer category include Burkina Faso, Djibouti, Gabon, and Togo. The three West African countries will also be influenced by the increasingly strong gravitational pull toward democracy taking hold in this subregion. The measurement scorecard for Burkina Faso, in particular, already closely resembles those countries in the democratizer category. Uganda also fits this typology, especially with the growing assertiveness of its legislature, media, and local government structures. However, the decision by Yoweri Museveni to push forward with another term in March 2011, 25 years into his leadership tenure, as well as the expectation of new oil revenues in the near future is a counterweight to these democratic tendencies. Nonetheless, few if any of the countries in this category, with the possible exceptions of Ethiopia and the Gambia, are likely to regress to the autocratic camp in the near term.

Within the autocratic classification, the preponderance of democracy inhibiting factors suggests that the dynamic of entrenchment is strong in the majority of these cases. Most starkly, leaders in 9 of the 10 countries in this category have been in power for more than a decade, with the average time in office exceeding 20 years. Nearly all of these regimes also exhibit strong limitations on civil society and media freedom. Six of the 10 autocracies benefit from high levels of hydrocarbon wealth, enabling them to bolster their support networks and resist external pressures to reform. Unsurprisingly, nearly all of these oil rich autocracies are also rated as among the most corrupt on the continent. This oil wealth, in turn, boosts economic growth in several of the regimes (e.g. Angola, Equatorial Guinea, and Sudan). Cameroon and Chad, in contrast, achieve the dubious feat of realizing low levels of economic growth, despite significant oil revenues. Regardless of economic growth rates, nearly all of the oil rich autocracies also significantly underperform in their development. In contrast, neither of the autocracies that have realized superior development outcomes have access to significant oil revenues. This mirrors a pattern seen across all regime categories — in no instance does a country score in the top quartile of development performance while simultaneously tolerating high levels of perceived corruption. This is particularly evident within the autocracy category, where the countries that are realizing the most development progress have maintained at least a median level of controls on corruption. Rwanda stands out among the autocracies for its superior economic growth, development, and control of corruption — substantiating its "performance-based" claim on authority.

While these indicators suggest the majority of these autocracies are well entrenched, there are exceptional factors and cases to consider. Surprisingly, 8 out of 10 of the governments in this category allow a degree of Internet access. This facilitates the exchange of information supporting their economic development, while opening a path for discourse between the government and citizens. Mauritania and the Republic of Congo further distinguish themselves by their relatively greater openness to media freedom. In fact, Mauritania's pattern of indicators suggests it could shift into the semi-authoritarian or even democratizer category in the near term. Swaziland, with a degree of Internet access, the lack of sizable oil revenues to buoy the regime in hard times, and stagnant economic growth, may also be more open to introducing legitimacy enhancing measures in the near future. Longtime leaders in Cameroon, Chad, the Republic of Congo, and Sudan, similarly, are likely to face increasing strains to their hold on power given their poor development performance despite the availability of major oil revenues. The high levels of perceived corruption in each of these regimes, moreover, are likely to further stoke public antipathy. Finally, 4 of the 10 autocracies are experiencing high levels of inflation, reflecting another source of instability that these regimes must navigate.

In short, while the factors considered here are by no means comprehensive for what is a highly complex process subject to numerous contingencies and context specific influences, the range of forces shaping democratic development in Africa suggests that the coming years will continue to see continued dynamism in governance norms. These dynamics mostly point to upward shifts toward greater levels of popular participation. This is particularly true in the democratizer category where some six to eight countries could move into the democracy classification in the next several years. While less prevalent, cases of backsliding will also likely continue to occur for the foreseeable future, with one to two countries in the democracy, democratizer, and semi-authoritarian groupings being vulnerable of doing so.

AFRICA'S CHANGING GOVERNANCE EQUATION

After a period of stasis, Africa has seen a renewed push for democracy. This has been punctuated by the stunning departure from power of long-time leaders in Egypt, Tunisia, and Libya. While the drivers of Sub-Saharan Africa's democratic progress have been largely independent of the Arab Spring, the high-profile defiance these movements represent has had a galvanizing effect on Africa's collective consciousness and has helped jumpstart change elsewhere on the continent.

Still, there are significant headwinds that democracy proponents in Africa must overcome if they are to realize genuine transformations. Indeed, some may argue that since Africa has not seen the sustained, large-scale protests of Egypt and Tunisia (and elsewhere in the Arab world) that Africans are "still not ready" for full-fledged democracy. However, the analysis of this report suggests otherwise. Africa has made considerable if not linear progress toward democracy over the past 20 years. Moreover, even during recent years of seeming stasis, important structural factors, such as sharply greater access to ICTs, a growing youth bulge, a more sophisticated civil society, emerging institutional checks and balances, urbanization, and the expanded awareness of global governance norms, have positioned Africa for another democratic surge. Perhaps most powerfully, expectations in Africa for more robust democracy are rising.

So, while Africa has not seen dramatic, mass street protests, a democratic transformation is unfolding. African citizens are far less willing to accept unconstitutional changes, abuses of power, gross corruption, and state violence against the population. This is a major change from years past. This new attitude has been influenced by a key lesson from the Arab Spring — that citizens can and must confront excesses of their government if they expect it to change. The willingness and speed with which Senegalese citizens went to the streets in July 2011, after President Abdoulaye Wade proposed amending electoral rules such that a president could be elected with just 25 percent of a first round vote, is a telling indication of this change.

Given that democratic change occurs through sustained pressure for reform, a slow but steady unfolding of democratization has advantages relative to flash-in-the-pan protests that flare up for a day and cannot be sustained. The degree to which these transitions result in material advances in democratization will ultimately depend on the vibrancy and caliber of civil society networks within individual countries. These are the organizations that, experience shows, bind a society together across its diversity in order to maintain momentum for greater self-governance, transparency, and state adherence to the rule of law. These are also the groups that will need to draw the links between pent-up frustrations over basic socioeconomic demands — food and fuel prices, jobs, housing, access to water and sanitation — with the need for better governance, greater political representation, transparency, and responsiveness.

There remains considerable variance in the strength of Africa's civil society. Dynamic civic actors have been instrumental in promoting change in Benin, Ghana, Kenya, Mali, Namibia, Nigeria, Senegal,

Sierra Leone, São Tomé and Príncipe, South Africa, and Tanzania over the years. Even though it remains in its nascent stages, civil society was also vital in pushing for reform in the years preceding Guinea's dramatic shift toward democracy in 2011. Likewise, there has been maturation in the role and influence of sub-regional civil society organizations such as the Southern African Development Community (SADC) Council of NGOs that has called for greater oversight of electoral commissions and political inclusiveness in SADC "hotspots" like Zimbabwe, Madagascar, Malawi, Swaziland, and the DRC.[80] Still, civil society remains relatively weak in other countries where there is a degree of opening and the need for sustained pressure for political reform persists, such as Cameroon, the Central African Republic, the Republic of Congo, Côte d'Ivoire, the DRC, Gabon, South Sudan, and Swaziland.

So, while there is considerable institutional momentum for democratic gains in Africa over the next several years, these advances will not be automatic. Civil society leaders and reformist political parties will need to rise to the occasion to seize this window of opportunity, including articulating a vision for the future, prioritizing the types of changes that are needed, and organizing societies from the community level up to press for these changes.

The demise of North African autocracies in Egypt, Tunisia, and Libya in 2011 has had another indirect effect on Sub-Saharan Africa: it has undercut the viability of autocratic governing models. Egypt had long provided the model of military rule morphing into an ostensibly civilian-run government, though with the military retaining enormous influence. Hosni Mubarak had been a career military officer for nearly 30 years, rising to become Commander of the Air Force before being appointed as Egypt's Vice President in 1975. He then relied heavily on his military networks once he assumed the presidency in 1981. The model has been emulated in a number of African countries including Burkina Faso, the Central African Republic, Chad, the Republic of Congo, the Gambia, and Uganda. In the new era of heightened governance expectations reflected in the Arab Spring, Mubarak's weak claims to legitimacy were a major liability. This issue continues to erode the authority of the ruling Supreme Council of the Armed Forces, which many believe is aiming to maintain an influential behind-the-scenes role for the Egyptian military.

In a similar way, Tunisia's Zine El Abidine Ben Ali, borrowing from the East Asian Tigers, fashioned a seemingly stable autocratic model that was perceived to have delivered economic growth at the expense of political freedoms. In fact, Tunisia has been one of a handful of autocracies in the world that sustained strong economic growth for more than a decade. It is a model to which a number of Africa's contemporary autocracies and semi-authoritarians aspire, including Eritrea, Ethiopia, Rwanda, and Uganda. Still, the inevitable corruption, inequities, illegitimacy, and resentment that built up in Tunisia — in an era of rising expectations for transparency and service delivery — made this model unviable as well.

The political equation, therefore, is changing for the region's semi-authoritarian and autocratic regimes. No longer can they blithely dismiss calls for greater openness or punish opponents without incurring diplomatic and financial costs. With the globalization of communications, such actions are much more likely to gain the attention of regional and international partners and elicit condemnation. Uganda's heavy-handed response to the service delivery protests organized by opposition politician Kizza Besigye did more to undermine the legitimacy of the government than the controversial 2011 presidential elections themselves. Rwanda's trial of opposition presidential candidate, Victoire Ingabire, on charges of genocide ideology, revisionism, and terrorism, makes it hard to take seriously the government's claims of commitment to political pluralism. The Ethiopian government's continued constriction of space for civil society, including the business community, is driving away international investors that could bring much needed capital and economic vitality into the country. The army mutinies as well as protests against police brutality and service delivery deficiencies in Burkina Faso from April through June 2011, moreover, are vivid illustrations that the status quo will not likely be sustainable for even the medium term.

International donors, under budgetary constraints themselves, have also been more assertive in cutting aid or putting African governments on notice for government repression and ongoing corruption. Chad, the DRC, Kenya, Malawi, Uganda, and Zimbabwe have all faced such pressures in recent years.

Africa's semi-authoritarians therefore are being forced to recalculate their governance equation. They must either enhance the degree of domestic legitimacy they command and expand the distributional benefits of state resources or face the risks of growing popular resentment and resistance as well as international isolation. Hosni Mubarak, Laurent Gbagbo, and Dadis Camara are all contemporary examples of semi-authoritarian leaders who seriously miscalculated their staying power. And as has been seen throughout the Arab world, launching reforms once popular protests have already gained traction is too late.

Historical experience from other regions during the 1980s and 1990s suggests that leaders of one-party or military regimes that proactively led the process of transition to democracy, including broad-based anti-poverty programs, fared considerably better than those that waited for the forces of change to overwhelm them.[81] Cases that fall into this category are Chile, South Korea, Thailand, and Turkey. Specifically, autocratic leaders who led the transition were able to facilitate a gradual pace of change that allowed them to set the terms of their departure and guard their institutional interests. This included maintaining budget support for militaries and negotiating protections from prosecution for exiting leaders and their allies by subsequent political administrations. These leaders, moreover, have largely been able to live peacefully in their homeland with access to their personal assets, once they stepped down from power.

Authoritarian regimes that transitioned under pressure, often accompanied by economic crisis, were less able to shape the terms of their post-transition positions.[82] As a result, they were unable to protect the institutional interests of their parties and the military. Instead, they were more likely to be prosecuted for corruption or forced into exile. Such was the fate of leaders in Argentina, Bolivia, Brazil, Peru, the Philippines, and Uruguay.

Drawing on the experience of Africa's initial shift toward democracy in the 1990s, contemporary semi-authoritarian leaders could conceivably lead transitions to democracy and win competitive elections. Jerry Rawlings' leadership in Ghana is perhaps the best known example of this model. The long tenure of many of Africa's semi-authoritarians may disqualify them from running as candidates themselves. However, they are in a unique place to champion the creation of genuinely democratic institutions that they could leave as a legacy upon their departure from power.

RECOMMENDATIONS

While much of the world's attention is understandably fixated on the historic changes unfolding in the Arab world, the findings of this report indicate that the window for further political change in Africa is also open — and should not be overlooked. Africa has realized important democratic breakthroughs and advances in 2011 in Nigeria, Côte d'Ivoire, Niger, Guinea, and Zambia, among other places. Significant structural and institutional processes currently underway portend further democratic advances on the continent in the coming 12 to 24 months. Expanding access to information, education, urbanization, youthful populations, and the growing awareness of governance norms elsewhere are changing expectations African citizens have of their governments. These trends are also reshaping the capacity for collective action among ordinary citizens on the continent, which has long been tilted to the advantage of the ruling party elite. Access to lessons learned from reform efforts from other regions and parts of Africa is accelerating the pace of this change.

With over a third of the world's democratizers (more than any single region), the trajectory of African democracy will also have implications for global democratic norms. Similarly, given democracies' propensity for achieving superior development and stability outcomes, Africa's democratic progress will likely have wider ripples for the global economy and security.

Despite this positive momentum, advances on the continent are not assured. Changes toward a more inclusive distribution of power inevitably face pushback from vested interests. To reinforce these democratic trends, the following recommendations are provided.

Regional and International Partners Should Place a Premium on Legitimacy

History has shown that democratic changes tend to happen in spurts. This underscores the normative nature of political reforms. The demonstration effect of expanded political rights and civil liberties in one country changes governance expectations within its neighbors. Regional and international organizations, accordingly, have a vital role to play in upholding rising democratic standards in Africa.

Empower the RECs. The RECs have emerged as the central norms-setting institutions in Africa. Comprised of subregional groupings of states, they bring together neighbors with shared concerns and exposure to spillover effects when a crisis erupts in a member state. As peers, they also have significant influence. Africa's RECs have taken increasingly strong stances against nondemocratic behavior of member states. ECOWAS and SADC in particular have demonstrated a commitment to democratic governance by suspending members for unconstitutional transitions of power or actions undermining their respective regional charters.

That such actions are initiated from within the region gives them enormous credibility. Accordingly, when RECs take action against any member state, they should, as a matter of practice, have the full support of the broader international community. Parallel negotiations through outside states, the AU, or other bodies should be avoided. This significantly enhances the leverage of the REC while fostering unanimity of international action — a highly potent combination as seen in the Guinean and Ivorian cases. In situations where a REC is inactive in responding to a political crisis, the AU, the UN, or a contact group of countries should step in to fill this role.

The AU Should Demonstrate More Support for Democratic Change on the Continent. The AU has provided late and begrudging support to the spate of democratic transitions that have transpired in the region in recent years. This has not only opened a gap between the organization's actions and stated principles, but it also puts into question the relevance of the regional body. While the AU will always face the bureaucratic challenges of attempting to mobilize collective action among an organization of 54 members, the AU Commission must adopt a more assertive strategy for getting out in front diplomatically on matters of expanding legitimacy, citizen participation, and voice on the continent. This is especially so, when an African government is brutalizing its own citizens. By so doing, the AU can simultaneously enhance its credibility while ensuring it is on "the right side of history." Similarly, too often in the course of recent transition crises, the AU Commissioner has appointed representatives that did not have the democratic credentials to deal credibly with the problem. This, in turn, has exposed the AU to questions over its commitment to democratic solutions, especially when AU representatives are seen as undermining efforts of the REC. To enhance its institutional credibility, in future governance crises the AU should only appoint individuals to these roles with unquestioned democratic integrity.

Ratify the African Charter on Democracy. The AU articulated a compelling vision for the norm of democratic governance on the continent in its founding articles in 2002. These principles reflected the changing governance values on the continent and were intended to help distinguish the AU from its predecessor, the Organization of African Unity, known irreverently as "a club of dictators." To demonstrate their commitment to these principles, African states should ratify the African Charter on Democracy, Elections, and Governance. Ten members have done so, thus far, including South Africa, Zambia, and Guinea in 2011. Five more are needed for the Charter to come into force.

International Partners Should Align Engagements with Democratic Practices. International partners can bolster democratic norms by ensuring that their development and security assistance policies create incentives for democratic reform. African governments that are legitimate and accountable should qualify for a greater range and value of initiatives. As was done in Malawi in July 2011, engagements with democratic backsliders and unaccountable regimes should be suspended or scaled back. In addition to improving aid effectiveness, doing so sends important practical signals about the value of democratic progress. Naturally, these effects are amplified if international partners act in concert, as in Mozambique where a "G19" group of 19 international donors has coordinated engagement with the government, including the suspension of budgetary support in December 2009 pending specific electoral and governance reforms.

The relative decline in the use of aid to reward geostrategically aligned African governments combined with greater fiscal pressure on aid budgets makes this a potentially opportune time to advance such coordination. Greater consistency in the application of these principles by international actors will strengthen the incentives they are intended to represent — as well as minimize charges of double standards. This is a dilemma the United States and other leading donors currently face vis-à-vis their support for semi-authoritarian Ethiopia, Rwanda, and Uganda, among others.

Sanction Regimes that Use Force Against Peaceful Protesters. As part of a strategy that aims to incentivize democratic norms, when governments use violence against citizens demanding their political rights and civil liberties through peaceful protests, strikes, or civil disobedience, there needs to be swift and meaningful costs to the regime. Suspension of aid, arms embargoes, freezing of regime leaders' assets, travel bans on leaders and their families, boycotts of major export commodities, United Nations Security Council resolutions, the launch of international commissions of inquiry, and referral of leaders to the ICC, among other actions, have all been effective in various contexts and should be considered and implemented in an escalating sequence. Such tools should target not only political leaders but also high-level military and police officers who enforce violent crackdowns against citizens expressing their rights to free speech. Ideally, the respective REC and AU should take the lead in calling for these actions. However, political or bureaucratic delays may require international actors to initiate action independently.

Reward Positive Leadership. Regional and international actors can further bolster democratic norms by affording greater diplomatic recognition and status to African leaders that have earned democratic legitimacy. This may entail visits with democratic heads of state, photo ops, and other platforms that distinguish and promote leaders who are genuine representatives of their populations. Such actions may not require significant financial outlays but can have far-reaching effects on standards-setting. Similarly, every opportunity possible should be taken to recognize and honor African political candidates who lose elections graciously (rather than inciting destabilizing, often ethnically based, divisive tactics in order to maintain a claim on power). Timely appointments of these individuals to regional and international commissions, boards, fellowships, and "councils of statesmen" will have benefits for the prestige of these leaders as well as signal to other candidates the expanse of possibilities available once out of public office.

Plan for Transitions. This analysis suggests that there could be a number of additional democratic breakthroughs and advances in Africa in the coming years. Regional and international actors should accelerate their planning processes for these countries so that these external partners can be prepared to assist these transitions as effectively as possible. For instance, there may be legal or bureaucratic sanctions against a previous autocratic regime that would need to be unwound as quickly as possible. Likewise, young democratizers often inherit an economy in crisis, high unemployment, significant debt service requirements, and almost immediate autocratic pushback. Regional and international actors should consider the technical, institutional, and financial assistance they may be able to provide to help deliver short- and long-term democracy dividends and stability.

Support Negotiated Exits for Semi-Authoritarians. As semi-authoritarian leaders face ever greater pressure to stay in power, regional and international actors should ensure there are clear incentives for these leaders to exit proactively and respectfully. This will allow them an avenue to manage their own departure, sparing the country the trauma of a long period of uncertainty and potential violence. Such incentives will be more effective if established early when there is less pressure on the leader and international interlocutors. These arrangements may involve protections from international prosecution for certain alleged misdeeds. While there are limits to what can be overlooked and certain constituents will only be satisfied with justice on their terms, this must be weighed against the broader costs to society.

Strengthen Africa's Institutions of Shared Power

A distinguishing feature of democracies is their layers of institutional checks and balances. These institutions foster ongoing course corrections in response to constantly changing information, challenges, and external influences. This enables democratic societies to adapt to circumstances in a way that best meets their needs at any given time. As importantly, these checks and balances serve as moderating forces against the abuses of power and disastrous policies. Africa has made noteworthy gains in strengthening such institutions over the course of the past decade. Further improvements are required to sustain its democratic progress.

Ensure the Independence of Election Management Bodies (EMB). Too many African elections are tainted by the perception that EMBs, who are often appointed by a sitting president, are biased. To overcome this challenge, EMBs should become more technocratic organizations. The selection of EMB members should not be left solely to the discretion of the president. Instead, members should be selected based on their integrity and competency on electoral management systems. There are various formats by which this can be undertaken. One option would be for nominees to be vetted by an independent civil society body, such as the national lawyers association. There could then be a period of public comment before final confirmation by the country's highest court.

Invest More in EMBs. African EMBs are typically underfunded and understaffed leaving them unable to effectively fulfill their responsibilities, including voter registration, candidate selection processes, data management, polling agent recruitment and training, and voter and civic education. A key lesson learned from past experience is that EMBs are often formed and funded too late.[83] Instead, EMBs should be permanent institutions with funding allocated for elections two years prior to the event to enable adequate planning and implementation. EMBs' regular engagement with all electoral actors including political parties, media, civil society organizations, faith-based organizations, security services, and the judiciary can help ensure that each is operating with the same information, easing tensions and avoiding disputes.

Multisectoral Security Strategy. To ensure all citizens can safely participate in the process of selecting a country's political leaders, security considerations are required for the periods before, during, and after an election. Given the expanse of geographic coverage involved, engagement from the police, army, gendarmes, and other security agencies are typically needed.[84] Coordination mechanisms and a clear chain of command needs to be established beforehand to ensure these roles and responsibilities are coordinated and implemented effectively. The designated security sector entities should also have a standing reporting responsibility to the EMB.

Term Limits. Given the legacy of "big-man" dominance of the political landscape in Africa, term limits should be the targeted norm across the continent. Establishing or re-establishing this standard is vital to preempt "creeping coups" where elected civilian leaders become so powerful they usurp the powers of other branches of government. Maintaining predetermined durations of presidential terms will also reduce the winner-take-all mentality surrounding African elections, providing losing candidates and parties a definitive institutionalized target by which they can try to gain power.

Maintain Two-Round Election Process. A common standard for presidential elections with multiple political parties is that candidates are required to win at least 50 percent of the vote in a first round of voting. Otherwise a second round will be held among the top two vote-getters. This standard should be maintained and strengthened. Increasingly, ruling parties in Africa are attempting to limit voting to a single round or reduce the threshold for victory. Both measures give distinct advantages to incumbents, weaken legitimacy, and should be rejected.

Enhance Openness of Legislatures. Legislatures are citizens' representatives in government and thus are responsible for defending citizen interests in the public policy dialogue. Unfortunately many of the proceedings of African legislatures are closed to the public. To remedy this, legislative bodies should, as a matter of practice, open all normal plenary and committee sessions to the general population. Moreover, efforts should be made to broadcast these proceedings on radio, TV, or the Internet. This is consistent with the vision of making these bodies "the people's chamber." Doing so will foster greater public discourse and awareness on governmental matters and will improve the credibility of legislatures in the eyes of the population. Experience from other regions suggests that greater coverage of legislatures also creates incentives for representatives to act in the interests of their constituents and move away from bloc voting. Greater openness of legislative sessions simultaneously fosters higher levels of transparency in the conduct of government business through the reviewing of budgets, audit reports, and program evaluations.

Deepen Democratic Values in African Political Parties. Africa's political parties have the power to transform Africa's entrenched neopatrimonial political models. Parties are the training grounds for democratic principles and leaders. If political parties govern themselves in transparent, rules-based, inclusive, and accountable processes during their agenda development and candidate selection then they will command more legitimacy among their members and the population as a whole. These practices, in turn, are more likely to become the norm for the state.

Political parties are also the vehicles that link the interests and priorities of grass-roots communities to a national perspective. They are therefore vital institutions to enable popular participation in the political process as well as inform, educate, and unify societies across different regions and social groups. Facilitating regular study tours and interactions with more established democratic political parties in the region and beyond can accelerate this process. Likewise, establishing party platforms and hosting candidate debates on pressing issues are a means by which political parties can define themselves and help shape a vision for the nation.

Incentivize Positive-Sum Political Coalition Building. Africa's legacy of centralized political institutions is ill-suited to the highly heterogeneous composition of most African societies and reinforces winner-take-all, zero-sum political outcomes. To build on the value of consensus decisionmaking inherent in many African cultures, greater effort should be made to establish political designs that emphasize the inclusion of different elements of society or "consociationalism." The desired objective would be a positive-sum political system. Examples would be decentralizing more administrative and fiscal authority to local governments or institutional recognition of certain ethnic or regional interests (such as special voting districts for the Tuareg population in Niger). Similarly, to avoid elections becoming polarizing events that pit major ethnic groups against one another, electoral rules should be revised such that candidates have incentives to build broad coalitions of support within a society. Nigeria's system whereby a candidate must win at least 25 percent of the vote in two-thirds of the country's states is a commendable model in this regard.

Strengthen Crosscutting Civil Society Networks

This report has highlighted the indispensible role played by civil society in creating and maintaining the health of a democracy. While Africa's civil society has expanded considerably in recent years, further strengthening of this vital sector will be critical to realizing and sustaining further democratic breakthroughs.

Deepen Cross-Group Collaboration. While the number of civil society organizations in Africa has grown rapidly in recent years, they are often very fragmented, leaving them susceptible to cooption or amplifying existing social cleavages. Crosscutting umbrella organizations that build the organizational networks needed for civil society to contribute more effectively to the democratization process are vital. Networks will dramatically expand the dissemination of information throughout a society as well as cross-pollinate experiences and key lessons learned. Such networks will create forums where civil society organizations from various interests and regions of a country can meet. This has yet to occur or remains very limited in many African societies but is essential for building trust and organizational capacity. Identifying and pursuing issues of shared interest also enhances the consensus-building skills required of a democratic polity. As coalitions incorporate a diverse array of societal actors, they gain increased legitimacy.[85]

Strengthen National Identity. A constraint facing many African democracies is a persistently weak sense of nationhood. This inhibits the forging of a shared vision and collective action. Drawing on the farsightedness of Julius Nyerere, the former president of Tanzania, building this broader sense of identity should be purposively pursued. This may take many forms. Sports leagues, dance and cultural troupes, and national media programs are all effective tools for building stronger social cohesion. Particular efforts should be made to engage youth in this process. Youth are typically less resistant to intergroup partnerships. Moreover, as Africa's emerging democratic citizens, they will need this broader perspective and skills to thrive in this new context. Nationwide service programs that enable youth to travel to and participate in public works initiatives in different parts of the country can be a powerful formative experience that builds friendships and perspectives that last a lifetime.

Support the Expansion of Information Technology and Independent Media

The rapid and broad-based expansion of independent mass media and information technology over the previous decade has altered Africans' views of and interactions with politics and public affairs. Remarkably, this rapid change emerged and continues with little financial support from governments — African or otherwise — demonstrating the intensity of demand for information and communication and the vibrancy of private investors and companies. As the ICT sector further evolves, it can be strengthened by targeted assistance, thereby further reinforcing its positive influence on democracy trends in Africa.

Strengthen Media and Technology Business Practices. Many Africans have already earned fortunes launching successful media and technology companies. Still, market research about African media consumers and information technology users is sorely lacking, making it much more difficult for new players to launch start ups or for established outlets to expand their work, make acquisitions, or pursue mergers. In these cases, market research in rural or underserved areas should be viewed as a public good worthy of assistance so as to feed growth in the media and tech sectors. Business management skills are also often very weak, leading many promising media and tech ventures to founder. Such skills are all the more critical given the rapidly changing nature of the media sector globally. Focused skills-development programs for managing funds and personnel as well as developing and implementing business strategies are needed.

Prioritize Diverse and Independent Media Ownership. Maintaining a diverse and dynamic business playing field will be critical to ensuring that the media and technology sectors remain independent and not aligned with the narrow interests of influential individuals or political parties. Regional groups such as the West Africa Media Development Fund and Southern Africa Media Development Fund have developed viable business models for identifying and assessing independent media ventures and providing them with seed funding and loans. Their portfolios and lending capacity could be expanded and similar organizations established elsewhere. Venture capitalists should also be incentivized and supported to make investments. Regulations should be instituted to prevent the dominance of too few companies or owners. As part of this, media and technology companies should also be required to disclose how they are funded to ensure that no person or entity, perhaps associated with politics or the government, is able surreptitiously to exert pressure or skew reporting.

Strengthen Professional Bodies to Organize and Self-Regulate. Professional media and technology associations are rare in Africa, and those that exist are weak and have limited capacity. Accordingly, priority should be given to strengthening African editors' and journalists' guilds, broadcaster associations, national community radio networks, technology collectives, and similar professional bodies. Without such groups, media professionals are unable to self-regulate the sector by setting standards for reporting and isolating media outlets that adopt unprofessional practices and disseminate inaccurate or incendiary content. In the absence of professional networks, media organizations are also less able to collaborate and negotiate with government authorities over an appropriate regulatory framework. In turn, government intrusion, intimidation, blackmail, or the blocking of online content as experienced in Ethiopia, Rwanda, and elsewhere, are likely to become more pervasive.[86] Professional bodies can also better ensure that freedom of expression remains protected.

Prioritize the Protection of Journalists and ICT Entrepreneurs. African journalists are still subject to frequent intimidation and attacks. Seventy-six African journalists have been killed since 2000.[87] Many of these deaths did not occur in war zones but in comparatively peaceful countries, like Nigeria. Typically, murdered journalists have been found dead not out working a story but in their cars or homes with no signs of robbery or theft. Journalists have been jailed for writing pieces that criticize a president, but also reporting on corporate tax evasion or the security services' inability to prevent and respond to terrorist attacks. Mobile phone companies have been harassed, severely restricted, disrupted, or ordered to suspend or alter operations under questionable circumstances in Ethiopia, Mozambique, Uganda, Zimbabwe, and elsewhere.

International actors should publicly condemn harassment and intimidation of journalists and ICT entrepreneurs as an overt sign of democratic backsliding and authoritarianism. This should be reinforced with real penalties including sanctions and the suspension of aid. Similarly, since free and independent reporting is essential for transparent and sustainable development, donor assistance should be explicitly contingent on sufficiently open media and tech sectors and adequate protections for journalists.

Network Community Radio Stations. Despite the expansion of independent media outlets and communications technology, rural regions often continue to lag behind with slow, expensive, and outdated connections, if any. Community radio stations are the most common link in these regions, but they struggle to stay solvent and generate enough content to fill their program schedule.

African governments should accelerate efforts to build national Internet infrastructure, whether by improving cable networks, next generation mobile technology, or both, so that the benefits of affordable high-speed Internet can reach beyond cities to broader segments of the population. Community radio stations can then become key conduits of connectivity in remote regions by making more extensive use of mobile telephones and the Internet. This also enables stations to collaborate remotely and exchange content. Stations would benefit from being able to fill their programming schedule and improve the breadth and quality of their content. Regional associations such as AMARC-Africa (l'Association mondiale de radio diffuseurs communautaires) as well as national-level groups could be strengthened to facilitate such networking of community radio stations.

Strengthening Security Sector Loyalty to the State

The security sector regularly plays a key role in efforts to suppress political opposition and resist pressure to reform and democratize in Africa, as seen in Malawi, Uganda, Rwanda, Côte d'Ivoire, Mauritania, and other states where the military and police have intimidated and forcefully suppressed demonstrators and activists. These practices will persist if militaries and police remain unprofessional, unmonitored, and unaccountable.

Improve Educational Opportunities and Institutions. While room for improvement remains, the armed forces of Senegal, Kenya, Botswana, Ghana, and others have a strong chain of command, clear mission, and generally operate in a responsible, depoliticized manner. Such professionalism is due in part to the extensive military education afforded their officers at domestic and international institutions. These programs expose officers to democratic norms, demonstrate the perils of politicization, and focus their attention on managing national security as opposed to regime security.

Demand for such military education is strong across the continent. For example, courses offered by the Southern African Defence Management Network (SADSEM), an association of 10 security sector educational institutes in Southern Africa, are commonly oversubscribed. Assessments of SADSEM have determined that the curriculum "has provided immeasurable support for in-country actors facilitating the development of policy and transformation towards democratically managed security structures in the region."[88]

The positive impact of such training has been most evident during political crises and transitions. In Niger, for instance, officers overthrew a president widely viewed as acting unconstitutionally, yet quickly put the country back on a democratic track. This was at least in part due to the strong professional ties and values these officers had established through training programs abroad, including at the Nigerian Defence Academy.[89] Moreover, the professionalism and integrity demonstrated by the Tunisian and Egyptian armed forces during popular demonstrations were partly attributed to the extensive overseas military education and training received by their officer corps.

African governments and international partners should build on the positive role played by advanced military education. Exchanges and scholarships for security personnel to study overseas should be expanded. Additionally, more resources should be dedicated to strengthen and network Africa's military staff colleges to foster the dissemination of best practices. Resources must also be directed toward advanced professional training for Africa's police and intelligence agencies, which often lack even the modest opportunities available to Africa's militaries. Such investments may seem costly but are a bargain compared to the much more expensive, time-consuming, and destabilizing interventions they may avert, such as those in Côte d'Ivoire, Guinea, Guinea-Bissau, or Madagascar, among other recent examples.

Measure and Compare Performance. Performance and good governance within Africa's military and police could be further improved if assessments and comparative analyses of the respective security sectors were systematized. Currently, even basic objective information about the composition, professionalism, and performance of the security sector in Africa is difficult to obtain. As a result, assessments of respective national security sector capabilities are typically based on anecdotes and are subject to bias. A regularly updated and published index assessing the national security sector for every African country is needed.

The index should cover the military, police, and hybrid security institutions as well as their effectiveness, politicization, and accountability to civilian authorities, among other criteria. Such an index would allow African states to better manage and align their security resources, determine a steady pace of reforms, and laud progress where it is achieved. It could also be the basis of subsequent security assistance allocations. Avoiding a low rank or a "red flag" on the index would also be a powerful incentive for more recalcitrant political and security sector leaders to make genuine improvements.

Institute Balanced Recruitment and Promotion Policies. To better ensure that security sector leaders remain apolitical and free from conflicts of interest, recruitment and promotion procedures should be crafted to de-ethnicize the military and police and achieve adequate balance and diversity. This can prevent scenarios in which security personnel are more attuned to communal or cultural affinities than their responsibilities to the state and the rule of law. In Ghana, Parliament regularly reviews military recruitment drives to ensure that new cadets are drawn from all regions of the country.

Africa's parliaments should also assert themselves during the promotions and appointments of senior military and police officers as well as civilian defense officials to ensure that such decisions are based on merit alone. Additionally, African parliaments should require that security sector leaders disclose their financial assets and make them publicly accessible so as to render them less susceptible to the influence of patronage and corruption.

Reduce and Reform Presidential Security Units. The existence of outsized and highly capable presidential protection units in many African countries is an indication of misplaced priorities. These units are often large battalions, regiments, or brigades, suggesting that they are designed to repulse large-scale threats and conduct complex and lengthy operations. Protection of national leaders is an imperative. However, this should be based on best practice and not at the expense of police and military effectiveness. Presidential protection units, moreover, often operate in obscurity with little independent civilian oversight, contributing to weak professionalism in the security sector overall. As a result, these units are prone to drift and become a security liability. This, in part, explains the destabilizing role the presidential security units have played in Burkina Faso, Guinea, Mauritania, and elsewhere in recent years. Recognition of the importance of reforming presidential guards is increasingly entering the public discourse in Africa, such as in Uganda, where opposition Parliamentarians have pursued such reforms. Such efforts should be further supported and prioritized.

Conclusion

The ousting of longtime autocratic leaders in North Africa over the course 0f 2011 combined with democratic breakthroughs in a half dozen Sub-Saharan African countries have reshaped the contours of Africa's governance landscape. Underlying drivers of change, moreover, suggest that the prospects for further democratic advances in the next few years are strong.

Nonetheless, the legacy of neopatrimonial governing models continues to loom large in Africa. The concentration of power in a single individual serves to simultaneously perpetuate personalistic governance while stunting the development of political institutions needed to create checks and balances. Overcoming these entrenched norms is the central obstacle facing Africa's democratic transitions.

While riveting, none of Africa's recent democratic gains are assured. Revolutions are often the starting point and not the finish line of democratic transitions. The process of consolidating democratic institutions is typically decades-long. Experience shows that this sequence is commonly marked by gains and setbacks. Pushback from those who thrived from close ties to former regimes should be expected. At the same time, democratic setbacks are not necessarily the final act — but another step in the sequence of citizens learning their roles and responsibilities in a self-governing political system.

The legacy of "big-man" rule is also a central challenge for some of Africa's relatively more advanced democracies. Having grown accustomed to power and its seductions, even some of Africa's more reformist leaders have vied to extend their time in office. In the process, whether intentional or not, the effect is to weaken nascent constraints on executive authority and invigorate cronyistic networks.

The future trajectory of democratic governance in Africa, therefore, will be determined by the tension between these competing forces – the emerging drivers of change and the status quo concentration of executive authority.

While some have been disappointed that mass protests along the order of those seen in North Africa have not been replicated in Sub-Saharan Africa, this is a poor indicator of democratic potential. Democracy is not achieved by one-time surges of activity but by the sustained and cohesive political engagement of its citizens.

Key actors that will shape this engagement include civil society networks, political parties, regional and international partners, the media, and the security sector. By instituting greater constraints on executive authority, especially with regards to extending their terms in office, reformers can help strengthen incentives for political leaders to attain legitimacy, govern democratically, and leave power at the end of their constitutionally mandated terms. As this norm is deepened, semi-authoritarian leaders are facing greater pressure to adopt genuine democratic practices, or to facilitate smooth transitions from power. Indeed, one of the most revealing lessons from the transitions in Egypt, Tunisia, Libya, Côte d'Ivoire, and elsewhere pertains directly to the region's remaining autocrats and semi-authoritarians. Namely, those leaders who stay too long are likely to depart on terms considerably less favorable to themselves.

NOTES

1 A coup attempt by members of the Guinean military in July 2011 is an indication of the fragility of this transition.

2 Michael Bratton and Nicolas van de Walle, *Democratic Experiments in Africa: Regime Transitions in Comparative Perspective* (Cambridge: Cambridge University Press, 1997).

3 "Polity IV: Political Regime Characteristics and Transitions, 1800-2010," Center for Systemic Peace, available at <http://www.systemicpeace.org/polity/polity4.htm>. See also Ted Robert Gurr, Keith Jaggers, and Will Moore, "The Transformation of the Western State: The Growth of Democracy, Autocracy, and State Power since 1800," *Studies in Comparative International Development* 25, no. 1, 1990.

4 Based on trichotimized categorization of Polity IV's democracy score and Freedom House's (FH) aggregated political rights and civil liberties index. Countries scoring in the bottom tier of both indices (0-2 for Polity and 2-5 for inverted FH) are listed as autocracies. Those in top tier (8-10 for Polity and 11-14 for FH) are listed as consolidating democracies. Those countries in the middle tier or split between the upper and middle tiers are categorized as democratizers. Those with scores split between the lower and middle tiers are presented as semi-authoritarians. For Freedom House data see *Freedom in the World 2011: The Authoritarian Challenge to Democracy* (New York: Freedom House, 2011). Categorizations adapted from Joseph Siegle, "Supporting Democracy in Africa: Effective Aid Strategies" in Africa Beyond Aid, eds. Greg Mills, Holger Brett Hansen, and Jeffrey Herbst (Johannesburg: The Brenthurst Foundation. 2008).

5 Marina Ottaway, Democracy Challenged: *The Rise of Semi-Authoritarianism* (Washington, DC: Carnegie Endowment for International Peace, 2003).

6 Morton Halperin, Joseph Siegle, and Michael Weinstein, *The Democracy Advantage: How Democracies Promote Prosperity and Peace* (New York: Routledge, 2010).

7 Adrian Karatnycky and Peter Ackerman, "How Freedom is Won: From Civic Resistance to Durable Democracy," Freedom House, 2005. Joseph Siegle, "Social Networks and Democratic Transitions," *Developing Alternatives* 12, no. 1, December 2008.

8 Steven Livingston *Africa's Evolving Infosystems: A Pathway to Security and Stability*, Africa Center for Strategic Studies Research Paper No. 2 (Washington, DC: National Defense University Press, March 2011).

9 Zenobia Ismail and Paul Graham, *Citizens of the World? Africans, Media and Telecommunications*, Afrobarometer Briefing Paper No. 69 (Pretoria: Afrobarometer, May 2009).

10 *Measuring the Information Society: The ICT Development Index* (Geneva: International Telecommunications Union, 2010), 76.

11 Russell Southwood, "Are Mobile Phone Penetration Rates in Sub-Saharan Africa Really As Low As They Seem?" *Balancing Act*, January 28, 2011.

12 Enrico Calandro "Dynamic Changes," Fair Mobile Index 2011 No. 2, (Cape Town: ResearchICTAfrica, July 2011).

13 Mary Myers, "Radio and Development in Africa: A Concept Paper," International Development Research Centre, March 2009, 12.

14 Ibid.

15 Communications Commission of Kenya, Ghana National Communications Authority, Uganda Communications Commission, Uganda Bureau of Statistics, and le Comité de Régulation des Télécommunications du Mali. See also "Radio and ICT in West Africa: Connectivity and Use," The Panos Institute West Africa, October 2008, 38. See also Devra Moehler and Archie Luyimbazi, "Tune in to Governance: An Experimental Investigation of Radio Campaigns in Africa," (paper presented at conference Field Experiments, Institute for Political and Economic Governance (IPEG), University of Manchester, Manchester, UK, July 2008).

16 Calculations based on maps constructed by Stephen Song, available at <http://manypossibilities.net/2011/03/african-undersea-cables-a-history/>.

17 "World Cities Facebook Statistics," SocialBakers.com, accessed October 2011, available at <http://www.socialbakers.com/facebook-statistics/cities/>.

18 "Africa Facebook Statistics," Socialbakers.com, accessed October 2011, available at <http://www.socialbakers.com/countries/continent-detail/africa>.

19 Livingston.

20 "Mozambique unrest shows the power of text messaging," *Agence-France Presse*, September 7, 2010.

21 Ismail and Graham, 7-8.

22 Dave Opiyo, "Survey Faults Media Over Referendum Coverage," *Daily Nation*, August 24, 2010.

23 "Spotlight on Media Coverage of the Kenya Referendum Campaigns 2010," Peace Pen Communications, August 2010.

24 Virginie Baudais and Grégory Chauzal, "The 2010 Coup d'État in Niger: A Praetorian Regulation of Politics?" *African Affairs* 110, no. 439 (March 2011).

25 Sarah Katz-Lavigne, "Interactive Radio for Justice: Impact Assessment Report," Interactive Radio for Justice, May 2011, 4-5.

26 Ann Kidder, "From Short Wave Radio to SMS in Zimbabwe," Movements.org, available at <http://www.movements.org/case-study/entry/from-short-wave-radio-to-sms-independent-media-for-zimbabwe-adapts/>.

27 Lance Guma, "Zanu-PF Abuse Cell Phone Text Messages for 'Sanctions' War," *SW Radio Africa*, March 7, 2011.

28 Rukiya Makuma, "ICT Changing the Face of Country's Elections," *The Independent*, February 17, 2011.

29 "Govt Blocks Facebook, Twitter," *The Observer*, April 15, 2011.

30 "Uganda Government Bans Live Broadcast of Protests," Africa Centre for Media Excellence, April 28, 2011.

31 Akin Akintayo, "A Year of Goodluck Jonathan on Facebook," *Nigerians Talk*, June 28, 2011, available at <http://nigerianstalk.org/2011/06/28/nigeria-a-year-of-goodluck-jonathan-on-facebook/>.

32 Umar Jibrilu Gwandu, "Buhari Unveils Electronic Campaign," Daily Trust, February 24, 2011.

33 *Research Summary Report: Africa Media Development Initiative* (London: BBC World Service Trust, 2006), 30-31.

34 Mary Myers, "Voices from Villages: Community Radio in the Developing World," Center for International Media Assistance, April 2011.

35 Edward McMahon "The 'New' Civil Society and Democratic Transitions in Africa," in *Sub-Saharan Africa in the 1990s: Challenges to Democracy and Development*, ed. Ruhksana A Siddiqui (Westport: Praeger, 1997). Emmanuel Gyimah-Boadi, "Civil Society in Africa," *Journal of Democracy* 7, no. 2 (April 1996).

36 Joel D. Barkan, "Legislatures on the Rise?," *Journal of Democracy* 19, no. 2 (April 2008).

37 Joel D. Barkan, Robert Mattes, Shaheen Mozaffar, Kimberly Smiddy, "The African Legislatures Project: First Findings," Center for Social Science Research Working Paper No. 277, August 2010.

38 Steven Langdon, "Parliamentary Audits and Budget Review in Africa," Parliamentary Centre, 2004.

39 Barkan, 2008.

40 Langdon.

41 "Committee Homepage," Parliament of the Republic of Uganda, accessed October, 18, 2011 available at <http://www.parliament.go.ug/index.php?option=com_content&task=blogsection&id=0&Itemid=9&limit=9&limitstart=0>.

42 Daniel Vencovsky, "Presidential Term Limits in Africa," *Conflict Trends*, no. 2, 2007.

43 Nnoruka Udechukwe, "Resolving Political and Electoral Disputes in Nigeria," *Business Day*, November 24, 2010.

44 Gumisai Mutume, "Beyond the Ballot: Widening African Reform," *Africa Renewal* 18, no. 4 (January 2005).

45 J. Tyler Dickovick and Rachel Beatty Riedl, "Comparative Assessment of Decentralization in Africa: Final Report and Summary of Findings," United States Agency for International Development, September 2010.

46 Ibid.

47 Jesse C. Ribot, *African Decentralization: Local Actors, Powers and Accountability*, Governance and Human Rights Paper No. 8 (Geneva: United Nations Research Institute for Social Development Programme on Democracy, 2002).

48 Dickovick and Riedl, 2010.

49 Stephen Commins, *Urban Fragility and Security in Africa*, ACSS Africa Security Brief No. 12 (Washington, DC: National Defense University Press, April 2010).

50 "Regional Overview: Youth in Africa," Fact Sheet Developed by United Nations Economic Commission for Africa and the United Nations Programme on Youth, 2010, available at <http://social.un.org/youthyear/docs/Regional%20 Overview%20Youth%20in%20Africa.pdf>.

51 *World Development Indicators 2011*, (Washington, DC: The World Bank, 2011); UNESCO Institute for Statistics, 2011.

52 "Lions on the Move: The Progress and Potential of Africa's Economies," McKinsey Global Institute, June 2010

53 UNECA, 2010.

54 Both organizations were criticized for endorsing Faure Gnassingbé's controversial electoral victory just two months later, though.

55 Nicolas Sarkozy, "Je serai le Président de tous les Français," (speech delivered upon winning the French presidential election, Salle Gaveau, Paris, France, May 6, 2007).

56 "French court approves investigation into African leaders' assets," RFI, November 9, 2010.

57 Paul D. Williams, *Lessons Learned from Peace Operations in Africa*, ACSS Africa Security Brief No. 3 (Washington, DC: National Defense University Press, April 2011).

58 Amanda Lea Robinson, National Versus Ethnic Identity in Africa: State, Group, and Individual Level Correlates of National Identification, Working Paper No. 112 (Pretoria: Afrobarometer, September 2009).

59 Michael Edwards, "The Challenges of Civil Society in Africa," lecture presented to TrustAfrica, February 12, 2009. See also Gyimah-Boadi, 1996.

60 Joseph Siegle, "Governance Strategies to Remedy the Natural Resource Curse," *International Social Science Journal* 57, no. 1 (May 2009).

61 Laurence Ammour, "The Crucial Role of African Manpower in Libya's Domestic and Foreign Policies" (paper presented to the conference *A Strategic Look at Relations Between North Africa and Sub-Saharan Africa*, organized by the U.S. State Department and U.S. African Command, Dakar, Senegal, March 21-22, 2011).

62 Ibid.

63 Ibid.

64 International Foundation for Electoral Systems (IFES), "Election Guide Calendar," the Consortium on Elections and Political Process Strengthening, whose partners are IFES, the International Republican Institute, and the National Democratic Institute for International Affairs, accessed on October 25, 2011 at <http://www.electionguide.org/calendar. php>.

65 Nic Cheeseman, "African Elections as Vehicles for Change," *Journal of Democracy* 21, no. 4, (October 2010).

66 Judith Burdin Asuni and Jacqueline Farris, "Tracking Social Media: The Social Media Tracking Centre and the 2011 Nigerian Elections," Shehu Musa Yar'Adua Foundation, May 2011.

67 Halperin et al.

68 Transparency International. *Corruption Perceptions Index 2010*. (New York: Transparency International, 2010)

69 Halperin et al.

70 Ibid.

71 Mathurin Houngnikpo, *Security Through Legitimacy: Democratic Oversight of the Security Services*, ACSS Africa Security Brief, (Washington, DC: National Defense University Press, forthcoming).

72 Joel D. Barkan "Uganda: Assessing Risks to Stability," Center for Strategic and International Studies, June 2011.

73 Bruce Bueno de Mesquita and Alastair Smith, "Leader Survival, Revolutions, and the Nature of Governance Finance," *American Journal of Political Science*, forthcoming.

74 Peter Ackerman, "Skills or Conditions: What Key Factors Shape the Success or Failure of Civil Resistance?" (presented at the *Conference on Civil Resistance and Power Politics*, St. Anthony's College, University of Oxford, March 15-18, 2007).

75 Karatnycky and Ackerman.

76 Maria Stephan and Erica Chenoweth. "Why Civil Resistance Works: The Strategic Logic of Nonviolent Conflict," *International Security* 33, no. 1 (Summer 2008).

77 Ackerman, 2007.

78 Siegle, 2008.

79 Green (democracy-enhancing) and red (democracy inhibiting) categorizations delineate top or bottom quartiles within the region for a given measure. Leaders in power for 10 years or more are categorized as red. Civil society measure is based on Freedom House's civil liberties indicator. Media freedom categories are based on Freedom House's free, partly free, and not free listings. Internet access categorization reflects controls for per capita income. Economic growth measure assesses previous five year average of per capita GDP growth. Development progress based on 10-year reduction in infant mortality rates, controlling for starting point. Red oil categorization reflects five year average hydrocarbon revenues exceeding 25% of all fiscal revenues. Yellow oil categorization indicates known significant oil reserves though production may not yet be on-line. Inflation is based on previous three year average.

80 Constantine Chimakure, "SADC Urged to Isolate Mugabe," *Newsday*, August 10, 2011.

81 Stephan Haggard and Robert R. Kaufman, *The Political Economy of Democratic Transitions* (Princeton: Princeton University Press, 1995).

82 Ibid.

83 "Colloquium on African Elections: Best Practices and Cross-Sectoral Collaboration," National Democratic Institute November 11-14, 2009.

84 Ibid.

85 Karatnycky and Ackerman.

86 Robert Mahoney, "Protecting Journalists in Africa," *The Media Online*, May 13, 2011.

87 "Death Watch," International Press Institute, accessed on October 24, 2011, available at <http://www.freemedia.at/our-activities/death-watch.html>.

88 Elling N. Tjønneland, Chris Albertyn, Garth le Pere, Kari Heggstad, and Brendan Vickers, *Promoting Defence Management and Security Sector Reform in Southern Africa: An Assessment of SADSEM's Achievements, Impacts and Future Challenges* (Bergen, Norway: Chr. Michelsen Institute, 2009).

89 Achilleus Chud-Uchegbu and Cosmas Ekpunobi, "Army Dismisses Coup Plot," *Daily Champion*, February 26, 2010.

WORKING GROUP MEMBERS

Joel D. Barkan is a Professor Emeritus of political science at University of Iowa and a Senior Associate at the Center for Strategic and International Studies. A specialist on issues of democratization and governance across Anglophone Africa, he has held positions with or consulted for the U.S. Agency for International Development, the World Bank, the National Endowment for Democracy, the Woodrow Wilson International Center for Scholars, and the University of Cape Town, among others.

William M. Bellamy is the Director of the Africa Center for Strategic Studies. A retired career diplomat, Ambassador Bellamy was U.S. Ambassador to Kenya from 2003 to 2006, Principal Deputy Assistant Secretary of State for African Affairs (2001-2003), and Political Counselor in Pretoria and Cape Town (1991-1993) in South Africa during U.S. diplomatic efforts to promote a peaceful transition from apartheid to democratic rule.

Christopher Fomunyoh currently serves as the Senior Associate and Regional Director for Africa at the National Democratic Institute for International Affairs (NDI). Since joining NDI in 1990, Dr. Fomunyoh has designed, organized, or advised several international election observation missions, country specific democracy support programs in nearly 20 African countries, and the African Statesmen Initiative (ASI), a program aimed at facilitating political transitions.

Mathurin C. Houngnikpo is the Academic Chair of Civil-Military Relations at the Africa Center for Strategic Studies. Dr. Houngnikpo focuses on Africa's military history, democratic civil control of the security sector, and issues of accountability, transparency, and good governance. He is the author of several books, including *Guarding the Guardians: Civil-Military Relations and Democratic Governance in Africa* (Ashgate, 2010).

Edward McMahon currently holds a joint appointment as Research Associate and Professor with the Departments of Community Development & Applied Economics and Political Science at the University of Vermont. Dr. McMahon also serves as a Senior Research Associate at Freedom House. Previously, Dr. McMahon spent 10 years as a Foreign Service Officer with the U.S. Department of State and is the author of several books, including *Democratic Quilt: Universal Norms and Regional Organizations* (Kumerian Press, 2006).

Abdoulaye Niang is President and Founder of the Niang Foundation in Bamako, Mali. Prior to launching the Foundation in 2009, he served as Director of the Central Africa Office and later Director of the West Africa Office at the United Nations Economic Commission for Africa. Dr. Niang has also served as an adviser in the government of Mali. He is the author of several works, including *Globalization: The Key to Peace and Prosperity for Africa* (Ivy House, 2008).

Davin O'Regan is a Research Associate at the Africa Center for Strategic Studies. His research focuses on the impacts of Africa's changing information and communications landscape, among other topics. Prior to joining ACSS, he worked in the news room at allAfrica.com and has contributed to research projects at the Open Society Foundations and the Center for Strategic and International Studies.

Dave Peterson is the Senior Director of the Africa Program of the National Endowment for Democracy where he leads a program to identify and assist hundreds of African nongovernmental organizations and activists working for democracy, human rights, a free press, justice, and peace. He has visited more than 40 African countries since 1984 and has published numerous articles on African politics.

Oury Traoré is an international consultant currently based in Accra, Ghana. Prior to her current work, Ms. Traoré was the Regional Program Manager for the West Africa Network for Peacebuilding (WANEP) and served as a Senior Legal Officer with the Institute for Human Rights and Development in Africa. Ms. Traoré's clients include, among others, major international donors and regional institutions such as ECOWAS and the African Union.

Joseph Siegle is the chair of the Africa and the Arab Spring Working Group and the Director of Research at the Africa Center for Strategic Studies. He has served in a number of think tank, academic, and practitioner roles in a wide variety of countries around the world including in Western, Southern, and Eastern Africa. He is widely published on issues involving the intersection of democracy, development, and security, including *The Democracy Advantage: How Democracies Promote Prosperity and Peace* (Routledge, 2010).

www.ingramcontent.com/pod-product-compliance
Lightning Source LLC
Chambersburg PA
CBHW080536290526
45790CB00006B/2431